THE SOUND OF SITAR

MUSIC THEMA: BACKLIST

My Life. KHANSAHAB ALLADIYA KHAN
Translated and edited by
AMLAN DAS GUPTA and URMILA BHIRDIKAR

*Music and Modernity: North Indian Classical Music in
an Age of Mechanical Reproduction*
Edited by AMLAN DAS GUPTA.

More details on MUSIC THEMA titles at the end of this book.

THE SOUND OF SITAR

Subroto Roy Chowdhury

THEMA
KOLKATA 2014

THEMA
Publishing for Change

MUSIC THEMA

First published February 2014
© Thema 2014

ISBN 978-93-81703-34-2

Published by Thema
46 Satish Mukherjee Road, Kolkata 700 026

Cover printed by Hyam Enterprises
C-506 Lake Gardens, Kolkata 700 045

Printed at A P Printers
8/1 Gurudas Dutta Garden Lane, Kolkata 700 067

CONTENTS

1

Looking back

My first encounter with serious music was in 1961 at a big event in Kolkata organized by one Sudhangshu-babu who lived near Kalighat. As far as I remember he was a sitar student of the late Mushtaq Ali Khansahab and was keen to keep our authentic traditions alive. All leading gharana exponents were invited through my ustad, the late Kumar Birendrakishore. The only exception was the Maihar clan. Baba Alauddin Khansahab loved Birendrakishore as his younger brother, but could not come because of a mild brain haemorrhage for which was brought to Kolkata a few months later. Ali Akbar Khan and Ravi Shankar were both in the USA. Others who mattered were all there—Kesarbai, Mushtaq Hussain, Hafiz Ali Khan with his two sons Amjad and Rehmat, Ahmedjan Thirakwa and the Kolkata sitarist Mushtaq Ali Khan.

Had this type of a festival been organized today, I would call it 'miles away from mavericks.' It would have quenched my thirst for milk with *malai* and *rabdi* instead of the usual lassi substitute. Times have changed. There is now no full-blooded Senia Ustad Mohammad Dabir Khan to sanctify the opening of a festival with his rudra veena or put forth his arrogant feet to be touched by simple simon Alauddin Khan, thirty years his senior. This was normal then, and not arrogance till the middle of the century or even in the sixties, for he was considered a descendant of the adiguru, the khalifa; and as Alauddin Khan would put it, his guru's blood flowed in his veins. Gurubhakti and self-confidence were in interplay, highlighting tradition over achievement. It is said that eventually father Alauddin caught the runaway genius Ali Akbar by the ear and made him tie the shagird's thread with Dabir Khan, the last of Mian Tansen's descendants from his daughter's side. This was in Birendrakishore's Ballygunge Circular Road house. During the ganda-bandhan ceremony Alauddin Khan wept and said, 'Whatever I have—*tan*, *man*, *dhan*, I give to thee.' The newfound guru-shishya relationship did not function as they never ran into each other after this episode and always found some excuse to avoid each other. Ravi Shankar however maintained the 'sweet sounding link' once in a while, and was hailed, as always, as the good boy in the Maihar clan.

In 1961, I did not have enough money to buy the near three-figure season ticket for this Lalit Kala festival. Guru Birendrakishore promptly asked the organizers to give me a volunteer's badge to help listeners find their seats. Nine nights spent out of the house for music! Unimaginable in a respectable family, said some—as if at eighteen, I was already visiting the forbidden quarters. In the eyes of the conservative, there seemed to be an unholy relationship between Indian music and the garden houses of the affluent, which had become convenient rendezvous venues. My rebellion started then; and in conjunction with my kite flying, pigeon rearing and fishing, playing the sitar made me different but happy and contented with my world.

A number of things happened at the festival. My guru had asked me to stick to Ustad Hafiz Ali Khan. What I remember best is all that happened around him. Somehow I had the feeling that my guru considered Hafiz Ali as very original and the authentic bearer of the tradition of Ustad Wazir Khan. This was because his limited musical movements and the beauty attached to them somehow convinced Birendrakishore that Khansahab in his effort to preserve the authentic had chosen not to go beyond it. He asked me to keep my ears open and learn as much as possible. At that time unfortunately I did not have the capacity to learn just by hearing, but remembering his music now in the evening of my life I do learn, and learn much more. Birendrakishore, during that festival, spent most of the time trying to persuade Ustad Hafiz Ali Khansahab to increase the duration of his performance. That was a phase when he was not playing more than five to seven minutes at a stretch, and then start singing dhrupad compositions. This charmed listeners, for he had a brilliant voice. But then, his sarod sang slightly better than his also extremely *surela* voice. At this festival (probably due to my guru's insistence), he played a brilliant Bageshri for twenty minutes. The sarod sang without vocal interference and I have never seen such sustenance of notes in anybody's rendition till today. The sober and dignified thick bass effect and the sustained connectivity or *silsila*, one misses today in the comparatively shrill music that one is forced to listen to, survives like an oft-remembered dream, as also an oasis of solace.

The *jhala* moved like an orchestra where fluctuation in the string was more than balanced by Khansahab's brilliant left hand fingertip. Then, just as his son Amjad Ali Khan commenced, Kesarbai interjected: 'We have come to hear you.' Ahmedjan Thirakwa followed. The maestro smiled and said, 'This is also me.' More arrogant and fearless, Ahmedjan Thirakwasahab went on and on, relating old episodes that I would not repeat since I was not born then and hence could not have witnessed. One thing was clear— Hafiz Ali Khan was basically a melody musician like his pre-Alauddin colleagues, such as Abdul Aziz Khan on *batta been* or vichitra veena, Kale Khan and Nasiruddin Khan Dagar in vocal,

Barkatulla Khan and Amrit Sen on sitar. Those who came after him, like Bade Ghulam Ali Khan, Amir Khan, and to some extent Ustad Vilayat Khan, followed the same route preferring simple tabla or pakhawaj *theka*. This theka was beautified with limited ornamentation, and never disturbed the main performer, but enhanced the beauty of the melodic twists and turns.

A modern Zakir Hussain also seems to believe in this style of no disturbance, and when he is playing pure theka, he never necessarily butts in with distracting sound effects, or showing off in the last few matras before the *sum*, unless asked by the melody man to do so. Pandit Samta Prasad also played a peaceful theka when he played theka, and played his long *bols* only when his turn came. Others sometimes lost this balance and restraint and start overdecorating the basic beat at the expense of the main performer's melody. To these all time greats, orienting the music to the percussion, or making it tabla-heavy, meant going towards the *kotha* and towards the kathak dance. Carnatic music probably did not come within their scope of study. Even if they came to Abdul Karim, Khan or Aman Ali Khan Bhindibazarwale, they came in the form of a pentatonic Hamsadhvani or a *sampooran* Pilu called Kirvani in the south, which touched the soul, and the aesthetics the mind craved for. Percussion and rhythmic movements in Hindusthani Music were more associated with dance till the middle of the twentieth century.

HAFIZ ALI KHAN

Hafiz Ali Khansahab was the last pure dhrupad ang instrumentalist. He played the original dhrupads, and elaborated them by highlighting each part, viz. asthayee, antara, sanchari and abhog. The knitting of the melody was solid, but the duration of the elaboration in a concert shorter than the open *swar baḍhat* version where the melody weaving was free and not around a composition of bandish. Ali Akbar Khansahab told me that his father's gurubhai Hafiz Ali Khan was different, because he did not go out of the dhrupad song structure, and elaborated each line while keeping the original line intact. This is not possible for others, for the dhrupad talim backup is absent. I remember three musicians who could not stop raving in admiration, whenever they mentioned him. One was Abdul Halim Jafar Khan, the other was Mushtaq Ali Khan and the third was my other guru Radhikamohan Maitra. I am not mentioning Birendrakishore in the same breath for his love, admiration and devotion for him was of a different nature. Bimalakanto Roy Chowdhury recalls lovingly the new raag Khansahab played every day for Birendrakishore in the drawing room of their Giridih residence and how young Birendrakishore (better known as Khoka Maharaj) worshipped them.

Dabir Khansahab's uncle Sagir Khansahab came from Dubai and my ustad told me to stay close to him and keep my ears wide open. In his estimation, Wazir Khan's son, though not a pucca professional, was expected to hum the authentic style without any dilution, which I should imbibe and remember at any cost. He sang Megh with an emphasis or *nyash* in the shudh dhaivat. Later, when others expressed surprise, I could appreciate Nikhil Banerjee's shudh dhaivat Megh LP, which drew more on Birendrakishore's training and vocalist Amir Khan's gayaki in structure than the Maihar Gharana.

It was this association with my grand gurus that helped me learn the many versions of this monsoon melody. Megh can be performed with shudh dhaivat, played with komal gandhar, or even a touch of shudh nikhad while going to the antara, as done by Ustad Alauddin Khan. Megh can also be performed without either dhaivat or komal gandhar as Amir Khansahab's version, using the same notes as Madhmad Sarang, but a totally different structure is only possible with the genius of this Indore stalwart.

I also learnt from Sagir Khan that scotch whisky was only two rupees and four annas at the luxurious Firpo's and Grand in Kolkata, in his time, and they would give a full bottle for this and four small glasses! I was convinced then that Sagir Khan's love for the other things had engulfed his great musical legacy. His father Wazir Khan had realized it; and with the death of his eldest son Pyare Mian, he called back Alauddin and taught him in six months what would otherwise take six years of intensive talim to learn. It was this last emergency talim that he gave before his death—in the fear that the legacy would be lost—that made Alauddin Khansahab the most knowledgeable in ragas and instrumental techniques. This paved the way for Ravi Shankar and Ali Akbar Khan's domination of the Indian classical music world in the years to come.

I also met one Salamat Khan of Rampur in my guru's house in south Kolkata. Later I heard that he was a student of Nawab Chammansahab of Bhilsi, and since Ustad Wazir Khan was teaching the young Hafiz Ali Khan, who had come from outside his family, Chammansahab was doing the same in competition. Chammansahab's shagird offered to teach me some sitarkhani compositions which I was a fool not to buy. This was mainly because Hafiz Ali Khansahab did not like Salamat Khan's presence; and I was more fond of this grand and charmingly loveable man whose genius as a sarod player remains unmatched to this day. The strong human element in Hafiz Ali Khan was evident when he insisted on and started climbing the seep staircase of Ali Akbar's house to meet the ailing Ustad Alauddin Khan. I was witness to tears that fell freely, as both reminisced on Rampur and its music. It was here that Alauddin Khansahab went on repeating that Hafiz Ali had imprisoned the goddess Saraswati in his hands and could not be matched. Hafiz Ali Khan hailed Alauddin as an emperor of laya, who would exhaust not one but a couple of tabla players. This togetherness is unfortunately missing in musicians today, as also the range of feeling and naturalness in their musical expressions.

It was here that I first saw Annapurna Devi. She put the sari anchal around her neck and touched Hafiz Ali Khan's feet with her head. I found her charming and also beautiful in a way that was traditional and pure. I heard her music later and marvelled at the spontaneity with which one line followed another without any jerk or pause, totally in line with the melody loving traditionalists.

Ali Akbar Khan was perhaps the last great who carried himself with a humility that only supreme self-confidence and mastery can bring to a man. When he touched the shudh madhyam from a gandhar directly from the pancham, his whole character blossomed out. The soft-spoken giant echoed the pathos of a folk singer, the devotion of a kirtaniya and the silsila of the khandarvani dhrupadiya—all in one. An amalgam in a mould coloured by rigorous practice and the unplanned enjoyment of the good things of life, he was totally unaffected by what others were doing. Ali Akbar Khan's music has been the greatest influence on me directly or indirectly up to the madhya laya or medium pace. After this laya and in the faster passages, I have always found him mechanical and metallic in comparison. Maybe the instrument leaning more towards the sursringar in size and octave possibilities was not made with the fast taans of the sitar or sarangi in view. What Alauddin Khansahab had achieved was the fruit of tremendous practice and discipline, and of course at the cost of tunefulness and perfect application of the left hand fingertip. In this, the son reached ethereal heights which combined with sensitiveness, aesthetics and logical connectivity made hearing him a heavenly experience. I studied his musical expressions most intensely and came to the conclusion that he was his own guru. The greatest influence on him was he himself. I remember Dabir Khansahab's comment after hearing his Chandranandan and Gourimanjari: 'Whenever I hear a new raag, I can correlate it to some of our old unknown ones or the south Indian melkarta, but these two I cannot connect to anything I have heard in the past.' In other words this was Ali Akbar Khan —none could pick holes in his supremely creative and uninfluenced mind.

In a recent book the author quotes Annapurna Devi to draw his own conclusion that the Devi has the maximum percentage of Alauddin Khan's music. I am sure it is true, but I wonder which part: the alap or the gath baḍhat. As far as I know, there is no recording or evidence of her gath playing on the surbahar and since a large portion of Alauddin Khan was pakhawaj oriented, this part is automatically left out to make her 'percentage achievement' of Alauddin Khansahab lesser. To quote Ustad Ali Akbar Khan, 'I learnt from my father in his youth when he remembered every detail. When my sister started learning and was proficient enough to remember, my father had already started showing signs of old age. My talim therefore should be more authentic.' I do not know why there is this run for the original. Is our music static or is it being collected for the dark recesses of some museum? Music is not the work of parrots to be let out just as one has learnt it. It has to be polished, improved and even made contemporary without destroying the roots; and this requires a very high degree of efficiency, intelligence and aesthetic editing. It is dynamism and creativity that keeps our ancient music evergreen. Both Ravi Shankar and Ali Akbar Khan had this quality. Ravi Shankar looked up to Bhatkande and discussed and listened to other gharana stalwarts to bring about a standardization, to become non-controversial in raag interpretation which he succeeded hundred per cent. For example, when he played Sindhura he played the SRmPDnDS with the *komal ni* version instead of Alauddin Khan's famous dual N version which is SrmPNS, SnDPMgRS, and in which the Ustad has a 78 rpm violin recording. To indulge in a line of digression, Mushtaq Hussain Khansahab, who had access to the raag treasury of Rampur as much as Alauddin Khan and Hafiz Ali Khan, had composed a brilliant bandish in this Sindhura, combining both versions. Sometimes he goes DnDS in arohan and sometimes or finally, mPNS. This has unknowingly performed the triple task of standardization—enhancing the raag canvas and ending controversy if any in this beautiful evening melody rarely heard now.

Ustad Ali Akbar Khan beautified his father's sarod baaj. At the late Radhikamohan Maitra's wedding *jalsa* Ali Akbar Khan was remembered for playing fast, and fast only. The late Ustad Nasir Aminuddin Khan Dagar remembered his experience of listening to Ali Akbar as one in which he destroyed the boasting of Azim Khan in Bombay by his skill in laya and speed in all taals or rhythmic cycles. But then another Ali Akbar Khan emerged in the fifties. Those who had heard him before, noticed a sudden change. His music had become sublime and ethereal. It was more imaginative, sensitive and feeling . It was love and flowers, the green fields and the blue sky, and not his father's whip. This was during his stay in Jodhpur. Vilayat Khan was a frequent visitor, and the redoubtable music composer Jaidev, a daily evening companion. Bimal Mukherjee, the authentic Jaipur sitar player, recalled how just after he had joined the IAS, one fine morning he switched on the radio, and noticed a complete change in Ali Akbar Khan's approach to music. Maa Saraswati had come to heal the wounds of Baba's beating.

Azim Khan, Nizamuddin Khan's father, was an indomitable tabla player. In Kolkata he won applause and the young Jñanprakash was thrilled at the dexterity and clarity of this fast tabla player. The hard work of the father was transmitted to the milder son, and no one in my time could match Nizamuddin's skill in *laggi* and his beautiful and peaceful tabla accompaniment enhancing the melody.

Azim Khan's influence went on spreading in post-Second World War Kolkata till Masitulla Khan, Jñan-babu's guru and Keramat Khan's father, tricked him into a competition and with his 'Bhanumati ka khel', defeated him and made him his shagird was was customary in those days. This took place in the home of Masitulla Khan's patron and student, Raichand Boral, famous in his own right as a tabla player and film music composer. Jñan-babu remained with his ustad Masitulla Khan till the latter's death, but went on enriching his tabla repertoire from others whenever it was possible by learning or recording. As one of the proprietors of a leading electronics store in those days he had a tape recorder which was rare in post-Second World War days. Masit Khan's supremacy was established in Kolkata's tabla world with his 'Bhanumati ka khel' where half a dozen rhythmic cycles were maintained with all the limbs of the human body, keeping the contradictory beats simultaneously, yet separately. This feat was achieved by Masit Khan after years of sadhana and he used this to challenge others and win, whenever the situation arose.

Jitendramohan Sengupta, one of the persons responsible for the spread of sitar in Kolkata, wrote in his article, 'Ten Years with Ustad Enayat Khan', that he had heard about a musical fight between Azim Khan and his guru Ustad Enayat in the state of Tripura. Both claimed they were right, and the royalty did not have the competence to judge. Ustad Alauddin Khan, who was then visiting relatives in Shibpur in Comilla district, was brought in from the village nearby. Alauddin Khan was at first a little confused till Enayat Khansahab advised him to keep the *matras* or beats separately and not the taal cycle as a whole, not even in its division into four parts with the emphasis points highlighted. After two repetitions Alauddin Khan raised his hand and said Enayatbhai was correct and therefore the winner. This trick of removing matras during *sath sangat*, and then suddenly bringing them in, was Enayat Khan's forte. This trick was later used by Montu Banerjee, the great harmonium player.

I had never seen anybody play the harmonium so well as a solo instrument. Jñan-babu was also a brilliant harmonium player but mainly as an accompanist. Once with Bade Ghulam Ali singing, Jñan-babu came in softly from the backstage and took the harmonium from whoever was playing. After some time the maestro looked behind and smiled. What he mumbled was clearly heard by the audience: 'arey mei to yehi soch raha tha ki yeh ullu ka pattha aaj aisa khubsurati ka sath kaise baja raha hai!' [I was wondering how the fool has suddenly started playing so well today!] The world was innocent then, and there was no vendetta or hard feeling towards the person who was playing before Jñan-babu took over—it was just an affectionate reprimand for whoever was playing earlier, and fond praise for Jñan-babu.

HINDUSTHANI MUSIC IN KOLKATA: A LIBERAL STYLE IN THE MAKING

The Bishnupur gharana was already disseminating Hindusthani music in Bengal; but this was confined to Bishnupur, Krishnanagar, Santipur and some small towns in Bankura and Nadia districts. The legendary Jadu Bhatta who influenced Rabindranath from childhood and trained him with the choicest dhrupads of Tansen, was a disciple of Kasem Ali Khan, a descendant of Mian Tansen.

Radhika Goswami came a generation later and was rated among the best dhrupadiyas of the country. When the great Ustad Mushtaq

Hussain of Rampur made his maiden appearance in a Kolkata jalsa, Radhikaprasad Goswami, better known as Radhika Gosain, outshone him. Singing the same Darbari the next day, he brought out the subtleties of this raag in a robust Tanseni flavour, better than Mushtaq Hussain. Kasem Ali Khan Senia influenced and created a satellite gharana in Bengal, which had brilliant exponents. Folk heritage may have played a greater part than imagined.

Jñan-babu was a brilliant man. A versatile genius, he raised the status of Kolkata's tabla and tabla teaching to the highest level. With the late Jamini Ganguly, he systematized what Girija-babu (Girijashankar Chakravarty) had gleaned from the Ustads in the north and spread vocal music among the educated intelligentsia. Jñanprakash Ghosh also introduced the slide guitar to our city in the forties for hundreds to learn.

Jiten-babu's article was published in *Ananda Bazar Patrika* nearly fifty years ago. Newspapers then were music friendly. Now they are sensation friendly. The late Asoke Kumar Sarkar was himself a sitar player and had also learnt vocal raags from Girija-babu. Ustad Alauddin Khan played regularly at their Shyambazar residence where he introduced his grandson Ashish Khan to Kolkata listeners.

Their music group as students came into existence before Jñan-babu's house mehfils became famous, with Hiru-babu, Timirbaran, Jamini Ganguly and others performing. Ravi Shankar, for example, was to his Asoke-da, first Uday Shankar's brother and Alauddin Khan's son-in-law and only then Ravi Shankar. In the Allahabad Music Conference, this group went from tent to tent to find out if anybody could play *Pancham sawari*, a complicated rhythm cycle of fifteen beats which Hirendrakumar Ganguly had prepared to play for the occasion. Unfortunately no one could be found competent to take up this taal, till Alauddin Khan offered to repeat this cycle in melody as is usually done, with his would-be-favourite Hiru-babu as the veteran Ustad chose to call him.

A son of Bengal, Baba Alauddin Khan said, cannot be allowed to go back without performing. After this, Hiru-babu became the best known Bengali tabla player of his time and an inspiration for the young Jñanprakash. Directly or indirectly, Hirendra-babu's tabla playing remains alive today in the virtuoso Swapan Chaudhuri. From his childhood, Swapan trained with Santosh Biswas, one of the oldest disciples of Hirendra-babu. The professed amateur, not taking a brass farthing for music, did create problems during his national broadcast over All India Radio. The AIR, a body of the Ministry of Information and Broadcasting in India, is obliged to issue a cheque to any person performing for it, but Hiru-babu would not shift from his principle. Ultimately a solution had to be found by redirecting the cheque to charities. It is often said that this had its roots in a promise made by his father Manmatha Ghosh, a knowledgeable pakhawaj player himself, to his guru Abid Hussain during the formal guru-shishya ceremony that the guru would give him and his son whatever knowledge he had inherited in return for a vow that this would not be used in competing with descendants in the commercial performance market. This was a sort of protection for the sons and grandsons of the peshadari gharanadar Ustads. Hiru-babu kept this promise till death.

The founder of the Benaras tabla gharana, Ram Sahay, also a disciple of the ancestors of the Lucknow gharana stalwart Abid Hussain also had to give a promise during the *guru-dakshina* ceremony. This was more technical. Ram Sahay could teach whatever he had learnt, but without a tabla pair in his hands. It is for this that the Benaras school of tabla sounds different and leans more to the pakhawaj ang and keeps counting and calculation as the basis of their teaching. This was evident from the late Kishen

Maharaj's art of tabla playing. The last surviving descendant of the founder, Sanju Sahay has matured into a brilliant tabla player and manages the Ram Sahay school of tabla started by his father Sarda Sahay in London. I consider myself fortunate to have had the opportunity of playing with the great Kishen Maharaj as well as the descendants of the founder, Sarda Sahay, and his son Sanju several times. Krishna Kumar Gangopadhyay, better known as Natu-babu, was an extremely knowledgeable representative of the Benaras gharana. His vistar and baḍhat in tabla solo could be stretched at will, and yet remained novel, interesting and not repetitive. He, together with another stalwart of Benaras, Nanku Maharaj, who settled in Kolkata, spread the traditional Benaras baaj among young educated Bengalis. Kumar Bose of this gharana shines among the best in this field.

Hirendrakumar's tabla always remained different from others. Khalifa Abid Hussain had taught him with great care. The pakhawaj talim of the forefathers was transmitted to the capable shagird but not the personally developed tabla research. That was retained for the son-in-law Wazid Khan and grandson Afaque Hussain. Ustad Keramat Khan, the tabla genius of Kolkata, also thought the same and said that as a teenager he did not miss Hiru-babu's tabla solos to get a glimpse of pakhawaj and its gradual transition to pakhawaj oriented tabla in the root gharana. The Lucknow gharana was the first to play tabla. All other gharanas are offshoots of this mother gharana.

Badal Khan was among the pioneers who taught khayal and thumri in Kolkata. Being a very famous sarangi player, his emphasis was more on voice movements and detail. He taught Bhishmadev Chattopadhyay to move freely in the three octaves and with ease. Tayari meaning skill and laya meaning 'in beat and correct calculation' was the strongest points in his teaching, and not correctness of raag. When Bhishmadev became a disciple of Faiyaz Khan, too much emphasis on purity and correctness of a raag puzzled him. It was like caging a free bird. One who was used to putting all the seven notes in a Malkaus or a touch of komal dhaivat in Durga found himself imprisoned in the strict rules of the Agra gharana, curtailing all of a sudden his free voice movements. This made him lose his mental balance and seek peace in Aurobindo Ashram in Pondicherry.

In plucked instrumental music the protocols of teaching outside the gharana were diametrically opposite. The teacher would teach his own compositions more than the ones he had inherited from his guru. This system of teaching students and yet keeping them at a distance from the roots was common in traditional music training. The bara sitar, which had not yet taken the massive form of a surbahar, was made to teach those who were not of the family, but were devoted and served with sincerity. The Been or the Veena talim was kept for the sons and grandsons. The reason was purely commercial—keeping out chances of competition in the next generation and protecting descendants. I have seen Pandit Ravi Shankar too concentrate more on his own compositions than those of Baba Alauddin Khan while teaching, but here the reason was not commercial. It was more to see his own work popularized and his experiments accepted.

This teaching of the ancients or keeping them in safe custody within the family to give descendants a safe commercial passage failed after some time. The more talented shagirds took off in more attractive directions directed by individual genius or by sheer hard work and virtuosity. Imdad Khan kept the Senias gaping as his meend range and right hand power. The Buas broke this in the vocal music parampara of Maharashtra. Haddu-Hassu Khans' disciples, the Aleya-Fattu duo, now enriched with Bairam Khan

Dagar's dhrupad talim, opened an advanced voice technique in Patiala. Gwalior branched out into various tributaries, sometimes totally different in approach from the mother gharana and reached the doors of the immensely popular natyasangeet. In Bengal, equipped with the talim of Kasem Ali Khan, the Senia Bishnupur gharana kept alive their dhrupad repertoire in Rabindranath's raag oriented sangeet. Alauddin Khan's Maihar gharana with its percussion-heavy baaj branched out from Rampur with richer musical expressions. The Sajahanpur sarod survived in Radhikamohan's students. The Senia sitar with some Enayatkhani influence sounded more alive in Mushtaq Ali and his dozen students.

MIXED GHARANAS

Mixed gharanas with their richer vocabulary and more varied musical idioms emerged and probably reached their pinnacle in Nikhil Banerjee. He was despised neither as a rebel, nor as a mixed breed maverick. He was adored technically as the most equipped sitar player, playing Vilayat Khan's heavy taans and gamaks on an Ali Akbari Maihar base. Even his controversial raag interpretation did not prevent listeners from hailing him as the charming sitar player who played with natural feeling, and linked up phrases which held the audience from beginning to end in a trancelike rapture. No one spoke about raags. They spoke about his brilliance and his feeling; and the lingering effect of his sustained meends. His linked expansion of musical thoughts underlined with that feeling-oriented musical expression, which distinguished Bengal from other parts of India, charmed all. The same type of heart-touching musical expressions were also found in the young Prasun Banerjee, before he came under the wings of the Patiala gharana stalwart Bade Ghulam Ali Khan; in Bhishmadeb Chatterjee fresh from Badal Khan's training and before he started regimenting

himself to the discipline of the Agra gharana; and also the young
Ajoy Chakravarty in his struggling days, when no one persuaded
him to shed his Bengali roots.

JOHN GOMES, NIKHIL'S FIRST PROFESSIONAL GURU

John Gomes resided in Taltala. His house smelt of brilliant
Chittagong cooking. Chillies and garlic dominated the cooking style
even when they were not making vindaloo. John was perhaps the
only Christian ganda-bandha disciple of Ustad Enayat Khan. He
played with power and moved about the limited canvas the ustad
had made available to him—limited, but technically ideal for the
first five or six years which the student spends in getting control
over the sitar. John Gomes was an excellent teacher. He taught
many but could not forget young Nikhil's talent and hard work. It
was under his tutorship that Nikhil, an eight year old boy, won the
first prize in the famous All Bengal Music Competition and drew
the attention of those who mattered. His brother accompanied
him on the tabla. His brother, Shankar Ghosh and Shyamal Bose
studied the tabla with Jñanprakash Ghosh at his Dixon Lane
residence. Nikhil used to accompany his brother to Dixon Lane
where Jñan-babu stayed with Charuprakash Ghosh, his brother.
Charuprakash looked after the Radio Supply Stores which they
owned and became well known playing the Birinchibaba in Satyajit
Ray's film *Kapurush O Mahapurush* released in 1965.

Young Nikhil also took lessons in thumri from Jñan-babu, traces of
which can be found in his earlier recordings of Khamaj and Pilu.
Somehow John Gomes was unable to change Nikhil Banerjee's
right hand movement on the sitar. This was Mushtaq Ali Khan
hundred per cent! Maybe this was due to his first lessons in sitar
under his father, also his first teacher, Jiten Banerjee of Linton
Street in the Beniapukur area of Kolkata. Jiten Banerjee had been
a student of Mushtaq Ali's father Ashiq Ali Khan in Benaras. The

Jaipur Beenkar style of spreading the right hand in the Ra or the outward movement to the maximum was maintained till the end, making Nikhil's right hand movement the most powerful in the Maihar clan. Nikhil often justified his right hand as a natural movement, but when cornered in an argument as to what was the most scientific in today's sitar playing, he would acknowledge Vilayat Khan as technically his ideal and say that the fault was in his root, 'goḍay galad' as he would describe it. With his ten hours of daily practice, he was ultimately able to control friction with the second string, the joḍi, which till the late sixties had disturbed the cleanness of his fast taans. No wonder anyone who had heard his repetitive Desi played over AIR in the late fifties, would be surprised to find how practice had transformed Nikhil into one of India's leading sitar players in the late sixties. The goddess Saraswati had blessed him with both sur and laya and he was able to do the impossible. He superimposed a major part of Vilayat Khan's skill, virtuosity and khayal gayaki on a Rampur-Maihar Kharaj-Pancham sitar base. His two other teachers, Birendrakishore and Radhikamohan Maitra made him aware of the advance achieved in sitar movements by Enayat Khan and his son Vilayat. This awareness did not go in spite of his elaborate Maihar orientation. More because his actual guru Ali Akbar nurtured a secret admiration for Vilayat Khan's sitar.

THE SITAR OF WESTERN INDIA

I also noticed how great the Paschimi sitar baaj could be when I learnt for a short span of time from Bimal Mukherjee. Lineagewise, he was a beenkar gharana sitar player—the same as Mushtaq Ali but very different in expansion of a raag in all its detail. He would also make an oft repeated mokam, like the surela Mushtaq Ali, but stretched the music to work on a larger canvas. The meends were usually three notes like the rudra veena or even lesser, but continuous throughout, without pause, marked by a high degree of spontaneity—something only a master can achieve—even when the pulling of a string was not required; for example, when he stood at pancham in Mian Malhar he preferred to put his forefinger on teevra madhyam slightly pulled to pancham. At first I thought he was showing off, but later found that this was his unique style taken directly from the rudra veena—in short meends and raag mastery there were few equal to him in the country.

Bimal Mukherjee together with Munawar Ali and my guru Radhikamohan Maitra could be called Ustads in the real sense of the term. They could perform any raag however complicated without notice, even if you woke them up from sleep and asked them to start. A pandit is an epitome of knowledge and can answer or explain anything related to our music. I remember an interesting conversation from the late fifties: a student of Ravi Shankar was continuously referring to him as 'Panditji.' Bimalakanto Roychowdhury or Kochi-babu as he was fondly called, suddenly asked him who he was talking about—'the only person we know as Panditji is Jawaharlal Nehru and nobody else.' Things changed in the sixties and seventies; and Ravi Shankar was acknowledged as the pandit of pandits in music. One day I cornered Kochi-da, determined to get an answer. How would you rate Ravi Shankar as a musician? The fullblooded ganda-bandha Enayatkhani would not reply. I also would not stop pestering him for an answer. Ultimately he smiled and said , 'Arey baba, had he not been brilliant would we have discussed him every day for hours?'

Nowadays Ustad and Pundit are freely used by barbers, cooks, egg-mutton roll makers, and musicians similar in rank. Most of them wear gorgeous, decorated, starched and ironed kurtas and carry briefcases instead of their musical instruments and are attached more to the computer in spite of their spelling errors.

Imrat Khan called them 'representatives of the cassette gharana.' Not cassettes, I corrected him, MP3!

Bimal Mukherjee would go to the other extreme. With his beautiful raagdari, he could not reach out to a large audience as he should have. These intensive talimprapta musicians are so obsessed with their own music that they rarely hear others except with sneering contempt. In the process, they are left with a total ignorance of the magnificience of tone which today's sitar has achieved in the Hiren Roy art of sitar making. A slight suppression of the main string in a slight thick tabli sitar (tabli is the round wooden plate which covers the open side of the cut natural gourd) can do wonders to the tone of the sitar, giving it a roundness and sustenance both in meend and fret playing. In musical content Bimal Mukherjee was brilliant in alap baḍhat or expansion; but like beenkars he would never give any importance to the role of the percussion and the thrill of rhythmic variations that the listeners had got used to. Ustad Alauddin Khan and his shagirds had changed the listeners' taste and they always wanted the excitement of the percussion *ang*. Radhikamohan was the only performer on plucked instruments outside Maihar who had learnt over five hundred pakhawaj subdivisions and varied his jaba bol banisi and his toḍas to be able to land in the *sum* with the spontaneity and confidence of a Ustad. 'Go and learn jaba variation from him,' Ali Akbar Khan often told his son Dhyanesh, who is no more. Amjad Ali Khan has also acquired tremendous control over laya and laya divisions and in this respect immensely enriched his gharana legacy.

Mohammad Ameer Khan's jaba variations found in Radhu-babu a meticulous editor and able exponent, totally free from the usual percussion fright of the gharanadar melody-laden musician. He met Ustad Alauddin as a young man, played with him at the Allahabad Music Conference and frequently visited the Ustad at

Hotel Cecil near Amherst Street during his frequent trips from Maihar to Kolkata. On one such visit, Radhu-babu told me, he heard Ravi Shankar play. This was before Ravi-jis concert career had commenced. Nervous as he was, Ravi-ji faltered thrice in the Bhairavi he played and went slightly off key. The Ustad, known for his bad temper, clawed the bed cover on which he sat. Ravi-ji was never able to forget this, said Radhu-babu, but did not forget to add that Ravi Shankar's Mian ki Todi was the best he had heard in this raag and was charmed. Commercial enmity among musicians in the latter half of the twentieth century was never an amalgam of the good and the bad as before. It was always one of the two.

Such close relationship with Alauddin Khansahab must have had some influence and Radhika-babu's heavy and weighty right hand does remind us of the Maihar-Bengal sarodist. In composition treasury, Radhu-babu was second to none. He had in his collection his parent gharana and Sahajad Mohammad, the best of Rezakhani, and Ferozkhani. The latter was slower and more left hand ornamented. It is often believed that Abdulla Khan's teacher Murad Ali Khan, the composition treasurer of the gharana, for some family rift directed his entire repertoire towards Abdulla Khan and Mohammad Ameer Khan (whom he adopted as a son).

Banikantha Mukherjee, who according to Ustad Hafiz Ali Khan, was extremely talented, worked in the Electric Supply Corporation, and could not do much research on what he got from his Ustad Ameer Khan. Timirbaran, the other extremely talented student, went away to Alauddin Khansahab, and with his mixed talim base, experimented successfully with orchestration and film music. Ravi Shankar had been influenced by Timirbaran in his own efforts at orchestration. Naushad worked under him in Lahore, in film music. Therefore I cannot mark Timirbaran as a runaway failure but one who had chosen his own course and did what he wanted to do. A pioneer in whatever has been achieved in Indian orchestration, he was happy doing his chosen job.

I have used the phrase 'efforts at orchestration', because Indian music is essentially melodic and not harmonic; and improvised. Any comparison with western orchestration will merely reveal its infantile and elementary nature. Timirbaran did some very useful pioneering work at combining instruments and was miles ahead of his guru Ustad Alauddin Khan and his amateurish Maihar band. If Turkish orchestra is kept as a model we can praise these efforts, but if you play Bach, Mozart, Beethoven or Brahms or even a second class European college orchestra, we can at best call them a slight improvement on the mono-pitched Jatra ensemble. My personal friend Ananda Shankar understood this and his work had a soothing effect, for he made each instrument perform with its solo beauty to the full. It is a pity he died so early. In the absence of harmony (systematic change of pitch) and counterpoint, one misses the waves of the third dimension.

RADHIKAMOHAN MAITRA: PURIFICATION OF THE SAROD TRADITION

Radhikamohan Maitra remained true to traditional gharanadar music and remained the sole representative of the Mohammad Ameer Khan sarod style. He had the time and the education to systematize the entire gharana *baaj* and edit the hundreds of compositions his guru had lovingly taught him. He also purified under his second guru Mohammad Dabir Khan whatever he had learnt before. This purification in the authenticity of Tansen's family music inheritance is nothing new. Ghulam Ali Bangash used to visit Rampur Basat Khan, for precisely the same purpose. Niyamatulla, father of Keramatulla and Kukuv Khan, did the same. So did Bairam Khan Dagar, to enrich the Dagar gharana. No wonder if we study, for example, a composition in Jhinjhoti we find strange similarities in all the sarod gharanas including Maihar—the link being Dabir Khan's grandfather Wazir Khan of Rampur or Bahadur Hussain, or Basat Khan himself, or his two sons Jafar Khan and Pyare Khan.

Most of the recognized gharanas of instrumental music had at some point of time drawn on the treasures of these descendants of Mian Tansen. In the absence of radio, television, and an adequate decipherable notation system, the same composition took slightly different forms in different areas of operation, while retaining the general structure. The beginning as well as the concluding *sum* also differed in some cases, but a close study revealed some common characteristics and twists and turns, which only the same composer could have given.

BABBU SAHAB

In the first three years of my association with Indian music I met Rahmat Ali Khan or Babbu sahab as his friends fondly called him. He was the first son of Hafiz Ali Khansahab through his second wife whom he married at a relatively older age after the demise of his first wife. The eldest son from his first wife, Mubarak Ali, a strikingly handsome man, was also a relatively good sarod player but was eclipsed by Ahmed Ali's brilliance and virituosity. Ahmed Ali was Nabbu Khan's son, and could play sitar or khayal *ekhara* taans at tremendous speed and clarity in his fretless sarod. He became rather eccentric in his later years. All these brothers and cousins except the youngest Amjad Ali were tabla shy and felt uneasy whenever the percussion started. Amjad Ali on the contrary, did a lot of research in tabla and could if necessary, make his music percussion-heavy as anybody in any gharana.

Rahmat Ali is fondly missed by the Delhi elite of yesteryears for his large-heartedness and goodness. I last met him in Bhopal where

he worked as a staff artist of All India Radio. Diabetes had by
then taken away most of the brightness he was known to have.
He waved from the wings of Rabindra Bhavan while I was
performing and took me to his home for dinner. He offered me a
Chivas Regal from a bottle he had saved up for very special friends
and very tasty food he was used to from childhood. He died a
premature death, and with him died the little that was left of Hafiz
Ali Khan, unmixed and undiluted.

AMJAD ALI KHAN

Amjad Ali Khan came into the concert circuit in 1958. Everyone
who attended the Sadarang Music Conference hailed him as the
most handsome entrant into the world of classical Indian music.
S B Chatterjee, who was writing for *The Statesman*, the most
important English daily of the time, gave him a brilliant review.
Amjad was merely thirteen years old then, and was included in the
famous Kolkata festival at the suggestion of my guru
Birendrakishore who was then the president of Sadarang Sangeet
Sammelan, and Kalidas Sanyal, secretary. Keramat Khan
accompanied him on the tabla for the festival.

There was a gap of three years and I met him in 1961 at the Lalit
Kala festival of Sudhangshu-babu, where he created a sensation
with a beautiful Bageshri drut bandish. Playing a Gopal-made sarod
he played phrase after phrase with the spontaneity of a maestro
and I became one of his admirers. A few years younger than me,
he became my ideal performer. I followed him in all his concerts
here, and derived from his stupendous success the energy to
practise more, and become a performer myself. The friendship
that developed then, continues even today. My lessons with
Radhikamohan Maitra, Birendrakishore Roychaudhuri, and Ustad
Nasir Aminuddin Khan Dagar continued, and my admiration of

Ustad Ali Akbar Khan remained unaffected. It is possible to like rasogolla and sandesh as much for two separate reasons. I admired Ali Akbar Khan and Amjad Ali Khan for completely different reasons, as I did also Ustad Faiyaz Khan and Ustad Bade Ghulam Ali Khan.

When young Amjad Ali listened to the Ali Akbar and Ravi Shankar duets he found the two playing similar passages differently in accord with the capacity of each instrument. His dream then onwards was to surpass the limitation of sarod and play *ekhara* or one-stroke-one-note. This, he achieved by rigorous practice and keen aesthetic sense. In addition to what he had derived from his father, he had the Vilayatkhani model before him which he creatively put into his sarod, sometimes surpassing the clarity level of the sitar. This is possible for two reasons. The first is that the sarod jaba or plectrum is a wrist movement which is stronger than the index finger middle joint dependent mizrap movement. The second is the joḍi string sound which is always there when sitar is played. In sarod this can be totally avoided, bringing, in western music terminology, the playing string forward. In sarod he brought in all the khayal ornamentations vocalists boast of, like gamak, sapat and jamjama with an effectiveness which can serve as a technically perfect model to all musicians in all gharanas, vocal or instrumental. No wonder, the sarod players who came into concerts in the eighties and after are his copies, more than anybody else's. Amjad Ali Khan's greatest contribution to his own gharana was his concept of laya and its variation and subdivision. The even and odd rhythmic cycles as well as their halves are played easily and without that show of virtuosity which pains. They are soothing and the divisions novel and full of variety where no gulab pani is required to clean the ears. A new school of sarod playing has emerged, blending sitar, tabla, and sarod. This is Amjad Ali Khan's contribution.

If my first concert had been with the father and grandfather, the last, a few days ago at a marriage celebration, was with young Aman Ali Khan on the sarod. His Desh and Marwa was among the best I have heard. The pioneering work of Ustad Amjad Ali Khan has now been chiselled to even greater perfection and balance. Tonal variations have been more effectively utilized to aesthetic brilliance and the sarod is handled with greater ease. I am sure, the Amjad Ali Khan gharana will continue in Aman's students, who have started entering the sarod world. Amjad Ali Khan's rise to stardom was phenomenal. Within ten years of his childhood entry he was the most sought after star. In 1968 when Nishith Music Conference was organized by Badal Dhar Choudhury, pretty girls were already lining up for his autograph. Time has changed now. The golden age of our instrumental music is on the wane and young Aman and Ayan in spite of their brilliance will find the ladder to stardom much steeper and the gravitational pull much stronger.

MUNAWAR ALI AND IMRAT KHAN

There were two others who did not get their worth in our country, Munawar Ali Khan and Imrat Khan. They were both brilliant and had their individual styles from the 1960s to the 1980s. Munawar was overshadowed by his father. Since he was more Kale Khan than his father, the great Bade Ghulam Ali, he was dismissed by the audience as a rough voiced singer. The sweetness of his father made him appear rougher, and even today when listeners look back to reassess and acknowledge his greatness and individuality, he is not there to receive the belated applause. He died at 59, unable to understand why listeners do not understand his *riyazi* singing.

He was adored by a small but influential group, but only as a brilliant singer who could not become a star, with a mixture of sympathy and adoration. This was not his fault, for like any other entertainment, music concerts for most was an escape, and this they wanted to do in the Karun-rasa; for like loud laughter in everyday life, weeping in music was also the best escape. Shringara-rasa being the base of his singing, Munawar was not understood and appreciated as much as he deserved.

Janab Imrat Khan's sitar is solid but his surbahar is heavenly. He made the surbahar different from the sitar with seven note meends. If one goes up to five notes pulling, it is more a bara sitar for its low pitch tuning. The surbahar is special for its enhanced meend scope and its enhanced capacity and range when compared to the sitar, and not just for its low pitched tuning. Imrat Khan was technically the greatest surbahar player of his time and succeeded in even outshining his great brother in the LP records of Mian Malhar, Mian ki Todi, Chandini Kedar, to mention only a few.

Fame he received aplenty, as the second most sought after sitar player up to the nineties. He could dictate his terms abroad, not in India. Here he was sidetracked though he was first class, and was not discussed enough. He never got any award worth mentioning. Now he leads a quiet life in the Midwest in the USA and looks up to his three brilliant sons. But then many a flower blooms to blush unseen and lose their fragrance in the desert air.

BAHADUR KHAN

Bahadur Khan was another brilliant musician who passed away with very little national recognition. He was extremely talented and was supposed to have learnt the best that Ustad Alauddin Khan could give; for after all he was his brother Ayet Ali's son. Something went wrong however and his incomplete talim was completed by his liberal brother Ali Akbar Khan in Bombay. This talim, being concert oriented, gave him a style of playing similar to

that of Ustad Ali Akbar Khan in alap and joḍ whereas his sarod
tone and melodic virtuosity reached great heights, his laya talim
was miserable. We know Maihar as a laya-heavy gharana where
every melodic pattern has a laya count. Personally I have watched
Ali Akbar Khansahab teach his students in the USA. Each jaba
format is correlated to laya beat calculation and even the common
American student's right hand grip never misfires. Melodic
inaccuracy is sometimes there, but the right hand laya grip is never
lost. In other words, the student left on his own could be *betala*,
besura due to individual shortcomings, but never *behisabi* for the
guru's talim in gath baḍhat was impeccable. In such a gharana
how could Bahadur-da go wrong? Why was Ayet Ali Khan's son
totally indifferent to his uncle's laya talim? This has remained a
mystery. While on a tour abroad together, probably in the USSR,
Bahadur Khan would often ask Radhika-babu to teach him the
right hand sarod jaba calculation. Out of respect for Alauddin Khan,
Radhika-babu remained aloof, but acknowledged Bahadur Khan
as the most talented sarod player after his generation.

I have seen no one except Ali Akbar Khan play with so much
feeling as Bahadur-da. His left hand was superb and his
construction of alap and joḍ sometimes created such a spell that
even his indisciplined bouts with the tabla could not break it.
Radhikamohan Maitra considered him the most accurately surela
together with Ali Akbar in the entire Maihar clan. Bahadur Khan's
music in Ritwik Ghatak's films were as good as his cousin's.

Ali Akbar Khan's talim boosted his melodic roundness in concerts.
But then concert talim is a training in how to play, not a training
towards punditry. In his Colaba flat, Ali Akbar Khan used to
practise every evening with Nikhil and Bahadur on both sides
allowing them to enrich their melodic vocabulary. Whereas Nikhil
Banerjee would practise ten hours to polish up with Nikhil Ghosh

on the tabla again and again, enriching the melody in laya, Bahadur-da was quite content with sounding like his great cousin but without his laya variety and precision.

RECENT ENTRANTS AND THE FUTURE

A number of very promising youngsters came in after these Greats, contributing in their own ways to the world of sitar and sarod, but somehow one missed the personality, melodic richness and depth of approach which had stood out in the playing of the older giants. There was perfection no doubt, but only within a smaller range, and less varied. So much of it was pre-set and rehearsed that even a lay listener could foretell what would come next, depriving him of the thrill of the unknown and unheard. Once heard, the music did not linger and therefore one did not bother about when and where the musician would play next. The personality of the musician was submerged in the pomp of presentation.

Even at ninetytwo Ravi Shankar drew a full house at Barbican Centre, London. The individuality and personality of Ravi Shankar's music, together with the nostalgia for the happiness and pleasure which it had given earlier, dominated over his age and present musical ability. This thirst for it, even when the music is heard no more, does not lie with the dozens of Xerox copies in the market though chiselled to perfection. A Bhairavi or Khamaj thumri recorded by Vilayat Khan still gives more pleasure than anybody playing live and the Ali Akbar Khan sarod stroke still haunts those who have had the good fortune of listening to it when the master was at the height of his powers. Ravi Shankar's Bhimpalasi for a hippy festival still remains the best and most systematic Bhimpalasi.

Among those who entered the performance world after the seventies or eighties two or three were extraordinary in talent and perfection. They also remind us of a Vilayat or Ali Akbar and we listen to them more for the sake of nostalgia than for listening to them for their own sake. In other words, they have not added enough to make their own presence felt. Music has been made and organized from the stray crumbs of the all time greats—not styles. This has to be churned for a generation or two for the butter to emerge at the top.

Listeners therefore scurry for fusion music to hear something new, something not heard before. Even shishyas were different from their gurus before the forties and fifties. Vilayat Khan was different from his father Enayat; Ali Akbar was many times more soothing than Alauddin; Amjad was different from Hafiz Ali; Ravi Shankar and Nikhil were poles apart and different from their respective gurus. This was because their music was a product of intensive research on whatever training they had received—not a quick assimilation of remembered parts of the Greats in stage presentation, for some fame and money. The uncertainty of a scanty knowledge of the ragas can be a deterrent to creativity. If the doubt 'is this passage right or wrong' hangs on the musician, how can he create the new? He would rather stay in the safe confines of the tried and tested, to ensure applause. The maestros became maestros because they wanted to be different, each with his own distinctive style.

2

The musical scene in the twentieth century

In the beginning of the twentieth century, Indian music had its caste system. The Rudra Veena, an improved version of the ancient Kinnari Veena, the oldest of the lute group of instruments in the subcontinent, still ruled as the King. The veena players, or veenkars as they were called, commanded the same respect as enjoyed by the dhrupad singers, who were the highest in the caste ladder. This was because the veenkars knew as many dhrupad compositions as the singers, sometimes even more. Some of the veenkars were themselves dhrupad singers. The singer-instrumentalist tradition was very much alive in the twentieth century in Ustad Wazir Khan of Rampur, Nawab Chamman Sahab of Bhilsi, right up to Ustad Hafiz Ali Khan of Gwalior, and Ustad Vilayat Khan, who was alive till the beginning of the twentyfirst century, when he was still charming listeners in both the modes. Vilayat Khan was so infatuated by the khayal gayaki that at a monthly sitting of the Sadarang Music Conference in the 1950s he gave a solo vocal concert without the sitar. Things have changed radically since then, with commercialism and corporate patronage ruling over a highly competitive market—and no one prepared to humour a musician! It is now the other way round, with musicians, barring a few, trying to keep their patrons in the corporate business houses in good humour, and only too ready to dole out to them whatever they commanded. Vilayat Khan was the last king of our music world. No one would ever dare dictate terms to him.

Indian classical music in the twentieth century passed through three phases. The first phase was dominated by the native nouveau riches that had emerged with the operations of the British East India Company. In their attempt to emulate the earlier patrons, the hereditary royalty and the feudal overlords, they employed musicians without any knowledge of the music they performed. They were more interested in raising their social status in the first generation. In the second phase, the next generation became addicted to the music they had heard from childhood. By now they had matured to a point where they could distinguish between a mediocrity and a really good musician. But they would still prefer the fast passages on the sitar to the sublimely tranquil movements of the rudra veena. Thumri and Kathak came into prominence as they made the traders happy after a long day's work in the service of the goddess Lakshmi. As the faster paced sensuous music took over, the dhrupad and the veena retained their guru status, but had fewer concerts and less money. In other words, though the King Veena reigned supreme, its popularity could not keep pace with the less rigid khayal, sitar and sarod. The rich traders preferred to pay more for evening mehfils or concerts, but unless they themselves chose to be trainee students, they rarely shouldered the responsibility of the musicians' board and lodging. The concept of court musician remained confined to musician-landlords whose allowances were being cut continuously by the new rulers. There were now more self-standing musicians or freelancers in the real sense of the term, travelling throughout India, paving the way for the semblance of a raag standardization that is now in place, thanks to the efforts of Pandit Vishnu Narayan Bhatkhande. At least some raags like

Darbari Kanara, Behag, Yaman and Bhairav are now the same everywhere in northern India.

Concerts soon came to replace the court mehfils and baithaks hosted by rich patrons in their darbars. While the elders grieved over what was lost, actually it was a mixed deal. All the earlier kings and landlords did not have a feeling for the music they patronized and heard. Some of them treated the musicians like cockfighters and wrestlers. There were others of course like the kings and princes of Rampur or Betia or Bhilsi or Mymensingh or Gauripur who took lessons from the master musicians, gave them guru status and touched their feet in reverence.

The third phase in our story coincided with Independence in 1947. When India became independent and the zamindari system was abolished, democratic socialism was the song of the day. Concerts shifted from the large drawing rooms of the rich to auditoriums equipped with microphones. European style seating replaced the Indian baithaki style. This transformation was more evident in eastern India in contrast to Maharashtra and Karnataka where the Indian mehfil culture still endured. A new audience comprising a cross section of the postcolonial intelligentsia applauded and adored the successful and communicative musician. They ran after the performers with autograph books after a concert and touched their feet. The listeners then had the good fortune of listening to masters like Bade Ghulam Ali Khan, Ravi Shankar, Ali Akbar Khan, Vilayat Khan and Bismillah Khan at their best. The immediately earlier generation had heard the great Hafiz Ali Khan, Faiyaz Khan, Abdul Karim Khan, Kesarbai Kerkar, Enayat Khan and Alauddin Khan in top form.

In the third phase Indian music became international, thanks to the efforts of Ravi Shankar and Ali Akbar Khan. Their guru Alauddin Khan took pride in saying, 'My music goes wherever the sun and the moon shine.' The number of listeners also expanded in India with the more westernized well-to-do joining an already bigger group. The inflated auditorium and publicity expenses needed corporate business support, which initially came in the form of donations or small advertisements in concert booklets. Now sponsors were needed to shoulder the entire financial responsibility. They were usually few in number. Their support as in business was conditional and they naturally claimed the prerogative of choosing the performing artistes. It was only in rare cases that this selection was based on a trained appreciation of music; in most cases it was done without any knowledge of or even any serious engagement with music. Free interplay of supply and demand, or even survival of the fittest, or even public demand was replaced by a sort of oligarchy where the same group of musicians were repeated, often even in the same sequence at the command of the patronizing business house.

As an inevitable consequence, speed and percussion-thumping replaced the sublime music of the yesteryears and old compositions were replaced by wild improvisations often taking the raag away from its traditional roots. Not all was bad, for the changing environment laid emphasis on the editing of the music, the value of time-consciousness, and the importance of the tone, for the output was magnified by a powerful sound system that ensured clarity and captured more nuances and details in the rendition. However, if overdone, this had the danger of turning into a torture for listeners, who were sure to be devastated by its deafening impact.

ALAP: CONCEPT AND CONSTRUCTION

The singer-instrumentalists of the earlier century, and those before them had such deeply perceptive control and understanding of the musical idioms associated with the raag that they could reset the dhrupad song structure with the possibilities that their instrument, the veena, had to offer. This editing in sequence and speed was probably accomplished in the eighteenth and nineteenth centuries, when the veenkars studied the basic dhrupad compositions, drank the nectar of the raags, and formed phrases, very subjective, but forever honouring the distinguishing character of the melody— never crossing its own limits to digress into another raag. This raag-based swar-vistar or gradual unfolding became slower and slower with time, to give musicians the time to think, improvise and edit to perfection. This was alap, as it is known today—changing in ornamental content for the last three centuries, though not in overall structure.

Drawing on its associations with Hindu, Buddhist and Sufi traditions, this slow, structurally linked note-by-note development acquired a meditative and spiritual flavour. In their reverence for this music, some of the native princes or landlords would not hesitate to drop the pride of their lineage and stoop to learn this art of ethereal ecstasy. The patron, now mesmerized by the raag, turned student or shishya; and the court musician enjoyed the status of guru. This became quite common in the eastern part of the country, particularly in Rampur, UP and East Bengal.

Dhrupad singers of the Dagar gharana made this art of expansion, a major subject of research and development. For them, this was the wisest thing to do, as they did not have access to the vast repertoire of dhrupad as the descendants of Mian Tansen, the legendary singer at the court of Emperor Akbar in the sixteenth century. This is proven by the fact that Bairam Khan Dagar became a ganda-bandhan [formal musical initiation by the guru when he ties the ceremonial thread on the wrist of his student, thus inducting him into his gharana] disciple of one of them, two hundred years ago in order to enrich his family storehouse of dhrupads.

The nom-tom alap was slower, pleasantly repetitive, and more detailed; the note-to-note elaboration / swar-vistar predominated raag-vistar or raag elaboration, maintaining the relative importance of the vadi and samvadi notes and the time-honoured phrases associated with them. The importance of the predefined starting point of a raag known as 'grahaswar' started to diminish, making way for a less monotonous or pitch-heavy elongation, or a meditative, spiritual, yet aesthetically pleasing start. The Dagars set the trend of starting from Sa or the pitch, lingering there for a long time, and then proceeding to the grahaswar, for their opening phrase. Ustad Amir Khan and Ustad Vilayat Khan followed this style, and so did their followers; but rarely did they go to the grahaswar, unlike the dhrupad stalwarts, or their Agra or Jaipur gharana descendants. They were, it seems, bent on setting a new and easier trend in classical Indian music. Maybe they had tonal accuracy in mind, for as reference, the Sa was the surest way to check and be at the correct point, especially during fretless meends to follow, for vocalist and instrumentalist alike. As long as this is immediately followed by the grahaswar, one can have no objection, for first the Indian melodic character is sought to be established, and then the raag character. For example, the opening Sa in Mian Malhar could be followed by the grahaswar shudh madhyam coming up to the pancham, and dual nikhad to put in the correct Malhar flavour. A Jaunpuri could restart from the pancham in the true Jaunpuri grahaswar way after the Sa is established to put in the correct raag music flavour.

The problem arises when the grahaswar is totally forgotten theoretically, with the result that it is the Sa or the pitch all the way. There is not much of a problem in a raag like Yaman or Bhopali, but what about Kamod or Kedar or Hameer or even Desh and Jaijayanti! In sitar the jodi is Sa, the chikari is Sa. Why should we then play Sa all the time, and display complete ignorance of the grahaswar or starting point of the raag, logically codified in the

Tansen family manuscripts of the sixteenth century, and derived perhaps from more ancient roots? Besides, this type of baḍhat or expansion does not fit into some raags. Ustad Vilayat Khan, being a very intelligent musician, did not overdo the Sa in his LP *Night at the Taj* in Raag Chandni Kedar, and went straight into this sixteenth century melody that Birendrakishore Roychaudhuri of Gouripur had taught him, from the talim he received from Mohammad Ali rababiya (the last descendant from the line of sons) of Tansen. Mohammad Ali shuttled between the estates of Gidhaur in Bihar and Gouripur in East Bengal, to teach his favourite 'Khoka Maharaj.' Followers of Vilayat Khan fail to understand this, or may not even know what grahaswar is, let alone its importance in authentic raag elaboration.

In the twentieth century, the importance of grahaswar reached such a nadir, that it was rarely discussed. Today it is almost forgotten. Khayal, with its fast frequency ornamentations, started to destroy the slow meditative tempo and the system of the nom-tom alap of the dhrupadiyas. Sthayi, Antara, Abhog and Sanchari were simplified to Sthayi, Manjha and Antara even by the so-called gharanadar conservatives, and the distance from the framework of dhrupad went on increasing. Sthayi, which meant elaboration in the middle octave in uncomposed music, was followed by a lower octave in Manjha, and a higher octave in Antara. This was elaborated in vilambit or slow tempo, madhya or middle tempo, drut or fast tempo and jhala. Incidentally, jhala is a combination of the main string which lies on one side and chikari strings on the other side of the instrument. The other eight parts of Senia veenkar alap—thok, laḍi, laḍguṭhao, laḍlapet, paran, sath, dhuand matha—could be found in parts in some musicians, but never all of them together in any one musician in any one concert. In fact in the twentieth century—the khayal age—most of the musicians carry no memory at all of all those parts. The composed pieces in khayal or Masitkhani and Rezakhani in instrumental music followed a simplified three-part division. The four-part dhrupadi division survived only in the compositions of Rabindranath Tagore who could not forget what Jadu Bhatta had filled his childish yet shrutidhar ears with.

The styles of alap could now be divided into three: (*i*) dhrupadang alap; (*ii*) bandhan or kayed alap; and (*iii*) aochar alap at a slightly faster tempo.

The real dhrupadang or dhrupad-style alap wove around dhrupad compositions and the raag picture was clearly felt in seconds, the moment the first phrase was completed. Ustad Hafiz Ali Khan, Pandit Ravi Shankar and Radhikamohan Maitra were the main exponents of this style. Kayed alap could be compared with swar-vistar.

Bandhan or kayed alap sometimes charged up a tension in the more knowledgeable section of the audience, who tried to guess rightly or wrongly, what raag it could be. The Dagars sang in this style and Chammansahab, the Nawab of Bhilsi, kept the great Wazir Khan guessing raags one after another, in the court of Rampur. Faiyaz Khansahab did the same with Pandit Bhatkhande, when all his raag knowledge failed to recognize the simple raag Yaman which Khansahab sang with odd combinations, without crossing over to any other raag, not one day but a number of days, the same time every day. As a sign of respect, he asked his favourite student, S N Ratanjhankar to become Faiyaz Khansahab's ganda-bandhan student, as he found himself too old and fragile to start afresh.

Aochar alap, with a lot of ornamentation, was the strong point of the Imdadkhani gharana, as here somehow technical virtuosity mingles with raag expression, and if correctly rendered, arouses a lot of interest. This type of alap is the easiest to appreciate, for even the lay listener would marvel at the technical mastery required for this not too slow ornamented movement.

Some khayal gharanas maintained the sobriety of the dhrupad from which they originated. If one hears aftab-e-mausiki Ustad Faiyaz Khan in his widely known 78 disc in raag Lalit, one can trace in his nom-tom alap the majestic structure of the Dhrupadiya alap. Here, the shudh madhyam is given its due importance and the system of the alap which came from dhrupad maintained meticulously. Other singers and instrumentalists had by then begun reducing the importance of shudh madhyam in this raag and preferred the teevra madhyam for the convenience of fast taans, drawing the character of this beautiful raag almost to the brink of that of the evening raag Purya Dhanashree in one part, and Gurjari Todi in the other. This was felt more in the fast movements within the teevra madhyam komal rekhav span among non-gharanadar musicians.

Whereas the Agra gharana took pride in being nearest to the dhrupad tradition, others like the Patiala Gharana, though an offshoot of the Bairam Khan Dagar gharana, with its conservative pride, took pride in its deviation from Dhrupad. Bairam Khan had embellished his Dagar family inheritance by becoming a disciple of the Senia gharana or the Tanseni gharana. His disciples Aleya Khan and Fattu Khan, better known as the Aleya-Fattu duo, went back to their native Punjab, after completing their training. Aleya-Fattu's disciples and descendants came to be known as the Patiala khayal gharana. However, while tracing their own origins, they would emphasize the influence of Haddu-Hassu (of Gwalior) rather than Bairam Khan Dagar. This may have been because one of their daughters was married to Bairam Khan Dagar, which resulted in a Haddu-Hassu influence. This influence is evident in the fast jod rendition of the Dagar brothers, in which the fast taans are intelligently superimposed on 'renanana renanana.'

With its emphasis on quick frequency meends, murkis, gamaks and fast ornamented taans, the Punjab or Patiala gharana did almost everything the constraints of the conservative dhrupad would not permit. Ustad Bade Ghulam Ali Khan was perhaps the only exception. He never budged from the conservative dhrupad structure in raag interpretation in spite of his superb voice control and command over more than four octaves. His Bhairav, for example, always wanted to go further up the Bhairav scale, the true Dagar gharana tradition, and not Sa re Ga as done by some khayaliyas. Dhrupad-bound Ustad Hafiz Ali Khan once told me that during his visits to Lahore before Independence, Bade Ghulam Ali Khansahab never lost the opportunity of coming to him and asking him about the talim he had received from Wazir Khan of Rampur especially in the char taaney of Darbari. [Here 'taaney' does not mean the fast movements as laymen tend to believe nowadays. It means alap ke taaney, where the raag pattern is more important than running on notes to make a show of one's practice and skill.]

Whenever Bade Ghulam Ali Khan came face to face with the Dagar brothers, Aminuddin and Moinuddin, he would get to his feet at once, standing up as a sign of reverence for the Dagar lineage of his gharana. Much to the discomfort of my friend Munawar Ali Khan, whom I adored as an elder brother, he was forced to tie the disciple's knot with one of the sons of Nasiruddin Khan Dagar—probably Tansen Pandey, who had converted to Hinduism and had settled in Kolkata. Like Ustad Ali Akbar Khan, Munawar too probably never undertook talim after his ganda-bandhan ceremony, which was a sign of recognition by his father, of the 'mother gharana.' Fateh Ali Khan and Amanat Ali, the actual khalifas of the Patiala-Punjab school, were always paying obeisance to Haddu-Hassu as the founders of their gharana, and acknowledging Bairam Khan as a link, and not as founder.

Fast taans without punctuation and point emphasis tend to disregard the relative importance of different notes, for all notes will appear equal in importance if sung fast, without the right pauses. Thousands of hours of painful riyaz are required for smoothness, uniformity and speed in performance, not raagdari. The melodic picture of a raag is in full display in the Dhrupad Veena style, where there is no hurry, and therefore the notes can be intelligently punctuated to give adequate importance to some, less importance to others, and the remaining given only the status of stepping stones. As a lover of music, I admired both; one for its closeness to the Dhrupad, the other for its distance from it. One lingered in the inner mind, the other was fun.

USTAD BADE GHULAM ALI KHAN

Though gharana-wise Bade Ghulam Ali Khan belonged to Patiala, he had a slightly different approach. I could see where he stood close to his parent Dhrupad gharana, when he stood still on a note, or even in his raag consciousness, in his fast movements. In my youth, I was charmed by his brilliant voice control, his aesthetic awareness and the extremely concrete interpretation of the raag he was singing. What impressed me most when I listened to him again and again in maturity was that he never decked out the slow portions unnecessarily with ornaments. In his Bhairav and Sree, for example, in the first five minutes of his never too long recitals, he would offer all the combinations dhrupad singers would proudly display as pure raag talim. His ornamentations started coming smoothly, and without a single jerk, only in the second phase of his recital; and when they came, they came rolling in, like waves. Before one had fully absorbed one, another rolled in. The listener went back home from the concert with the memory of his closing thumri, for his fast taans were too complex for the mind to absorb and retain.

Ghulam Ali Khansahab never sang too many raags at a concert. But whatever he sang was flawlessly correct from the most conservative angle. He could do anything with his voice and whenever he wanted to. He did not require any warming up. His conscious and self-imposed restrained singing clearly explained why he liked Barkatulla Khan's Senia sitar baaj and Hafiz Ali Khan's prized four golden alap taans of Darbari Kanara. It was a complete understanding of the motive of music, and the spirit of the raag which few, even among the famous, can be proud of. This flawless raag interpretation—at least in the slow portions— could also be found in Fateh Ali and Amanat Ali, direct descendants of the Aleya-Fattu duo, and direct disciples of Bairam Khan Dagar, who learnt from him not only dhrupads at fast tempo but khayals which his guru learnt from Haddu-Hassu. This could not be said of others. Once in 1961, at the request of Ustad Hafiz Ali Khan, Fateh Ali sang a number of old dhrupad compositions in a central Kolkata hotel room. This he did with such an abundance of khayal ornamentation and force that Khansahab was charmed and shocked. Charmed because the compositions were original; and shocked because of the rough handling of an otherwise sublime music form. Outspoken as the sarod king was, I was afraid that like Wajid Ali Shah, the nawab of Lucknow, after a gamak treat by Allahbande Khan, he would also ask for gulab pani (rose water) to cleanse his ears, and only retain the spiritual flavour of what was sung earlier.

The quest for speed, virtuosity and the desire to startle the audience with risky combinations had already begun in the 1930s. By the end of the century, equipped with a strong sound system, this acquired such popularity that it brought with it the imminent danger that it would gradually swallow up the very foundation on which raag improvisation rests. Clarity and speed had already had an upper hand by the middle of the century, both in vocal rendition and sitar playing; and there is reason to be apprehensive that the old 78 rpm, 45 rpm, LP records and CDs will remain as the only remaining guidelines to the correct interpretation of a Bhairav, Lalit or Darbari Kanara. The danger is compounded because Indian music cannot be understood or interpreted from notations alone.

ENHANCING THE PERFORMANCE

Faiyaz Khansahab brought glory to his gharana, not by destroying what was inherited, but by adding to an already existing middle tempo khayal, a slow nom-tom prologue which he borrowed probably from Allahbande Khan, father of Nasiruddin Khan Dagar. Performers and listeners alike were mesmerized by the magic of Nasiruddin Dagar's alap. The art of dhrupad singing was refined by smoothening the rough edges and making almost a spiritual hymn out of it, for the God almighty. Both Radhikamohan Maitra and Shyam Gangopadhyay, famous sarod contemporaries, agreed fully on this, though they were known to have their differences. Shyam Gangopadhyay went a step further and tied the sacred ganda-bandhan thread to become a disciple of Ustad Nasiruddin Khan Dagar. The training could not continue for long for the Ustad died young.

Faiyaz Khansahab derived the thumri influence from Moijuddin Khan in order to offer the audience a sweet dish after the main course. For this, he did not hesitate to hide behind a big almirah in Malkajan Agrawali's bedroom. While the baiji enticed the king of thumris to sing for her and served his favourite drink, Faiyaz Khansahab picked up the nuances of the singing style on the sly. Malkajan, better known as Malkajan Agrawali, had the same musical roots as Faiyaz Khansahab in the Agra gharana gayaki. Her 78 rpm record does not show much affinity with the aftab-e-mausiqi, probably because a large part of Faiyaz Khansahab's singing like the other Indian music greats was a product of his own genius superimposed on the basics of the Agra style.

The motto was enrichment of music at all costs and was a must for those who want to make it to the top in a world of gharanadar parrots reproducing verbatim what the guru did. Even the senior guru's coughing and clearing of the throat were preserved as authentic ornaments. Faiyaz Khan was more progressive and intelligent than his ancestors or the followers who came after him. His innovations were on a solid inherited knowledge base of dhrupad, which he embellished. It is for this that he was called aftab-e-mausiki, or 'the sun in the world of music.' Such an astonishing amalgam of dhrupad, khayal and thumri was nowhere to be found in the country.

It is wrong to assume that thumris are loosely knit because the flavour is light. They can also be tributaries from the dhrupad. Bandishi thumri, for example, is composition based, and does not encourage wild unbridled improvisation or crossing over to another raag and coming back. Folk music does seem to have an influence nowadays, but this is not so in the case of the dhrupad-based bandishi thumris. Ganpatrao Bhaiya sahab sang this structuralized thumri form and Girijabhushan Chakrabarty kept this alive in Bengal by teaching Jamini Ganguly, Sunil Bose, Jñanprakash Ghosh, Nutu Mukherjee, Biresh Roy, Naina Devi and others, who in turn had access to the educated Bengali middle class intelligentsia and taught them liberally. A monopoly of tawaifs and baijis, this form now found access into the liberal Bengali household where men and women sat side by side for music lessons.

In Maharashtra the liberalization of music, with women sharing the same space as men, had come in earlier, due to the popularity of natya sangeet and the combined efforts of Ustad Alladiya

Khansahab and Sawai Gandharva, in continuation of their gurus, in a more communicative format. In northern India this came a little later thanks to the efforts of Naina Devi, the granddaughter of Keshub Chandra Sen, the great social reformer. In Delhi, Ustad Hafiz Ali Khan, Mushtaq Hussain, Sambhu Maharaj, and the famous Dagar brothers taught at the Bharatiya Kala Kendra and raised the status of music and musicians in the city. The maestros teaching at the Kala Kendra would often have serious pedagogical battles, but all of these resulted in creating a stimulating atmosphere of true learning, exploration, debates, and a superb knowledge base. There was of course the occasional showdown among the greats in music as the one between Moinuddin Dagar and Mushtaq Hussain, as is fondly remembered by Ustad Amjad Ali Khan, among others, his musical grooming being under the same roof.

THE DAGAR GHARANA

Moinuddin Dagar, the older of the brothers, was an exceptionally intelligent musician. Observing the dwindling popularity of dhrupad, he decided to enrich his music presentation by putting some new wine in his ancient gharanadar bottle. He elongated the alap in keeping with the liberal trend of the times. Khayal taans were interpolated into the very fast joḍ. The joḍ itself was not common in that tempo in traditional dhrupad. This was therefore not only a novelty but a technical challenge to competing khayal singers, for the most difficult aakar taans were now sung with re-na-na-na, adding a very high degree of clarity and skill. The Haddu-Hassu influence by marriage of the great-great-grandfather and the khayal material in voice training inherited thereby may have been behind this novelty, in an eighth century music form continuously kept alive by additions.

If we go back to the gharana roots of the Dagars, we find two sources of gharana enrichment. Zakiruddin and Allahbande married

Bande Ali Khan veenkar's daughter and Haddu Khan's daughter, inheriting thereby the best of veena nom-tom alap and the voice training, virtuosity and the gamak-effectiveness of the legendary Haddu-Hassu. It was customary in those days to give music dowry to sons-in-law. The other daughter of one of them was married to Enayat Hussain Khan with a dowry of three hundred khayal bandishes, an anecdote widely known in the music world. Enayat Hussain had two sons-in-law, viz. Mushtaq Hussain and Nissar Hussain Khan (Rashid Khan's guru). Rabindranath Tagore wrote 'tumi kemon kore gaan koro he guni' after hearing Ustad Enayat Hussain Khan khayalia in Albert Hall, Kolkata (now the Coffee House in College Street). It is this enrichment within the raag picture and the subsequent enhancement of the singing format, together with the Senia gharana raag purification talim (introduced by Bairam Khan as a legacy of Dabir Khansahab's ancestors), that made the Dagar gharana the most complete in alap and dhamar singing.

On the one hand, the sublime approach of the nom-tom alap was made under the influence of the veena alap of Bande Ali Khan and elaborated further with an eye for perfection which can be achieved only if one works within a limited number of raags which the Dagar descendants did; on the other hand, they brought in whatever khayal could offer in terms of virtuosity, especially the earth-shaking robust gamaks for which Haddu-Hassu were famous, and put them into the old tradition of joḍ of the gamak and laḍi variety.

Thus the singing was infused with the sparkle of a good khayal— the sublime and meditative alap, with the dhrupad / dhamar composition suitably edited. Intellectual satisfaction was further enhanced for they were presented 'in the outer wrap of a dhrupad, coloured by the language of the gods.' Nasiruddin Dagar's legendary accuracy of notes gave the gharana a very high standard of perfection. This, combined with Allahbande's virtuosity in the Haddu-Hassu tradition, made the Dagars the best in old world singing. At about the same time the Senia obsession with instrumental music and raag variety made the coast clear for the Dagars. No wonder then, that the descendants of the Aleya-Fattu branch trace their origin rightly or wrongly to Haddu-Hassu Khans, much to the discomfort of those senior Dagars who survived till the end of the twentieth century. Bairam Khan Dagar taught Aleya-Fattu only the khayal they had received from Haddu-Hassu, together with the base dhrupad song to clear raag conceptions. No wonder when Allahbande sang for Nawab Wajid Ali Shah in Awadh, the nawab while praising him for his tremendous virtuosity and earth-shaking gamaks asked for rose water to soothe his ears. 'Gulab pani le ao,' said the thumri-loving nawab after paying them some extra gold mohurs, and started washing his ears. It was believed that Haddu-Hassu style gamaks could tame wild elephants and this was merely some absorbed influence from his wife's lineage.

Though Pandit Ravi Shankar's roots could be traced to dhrupads of the Senia gharana (his guru being a disciple of Wazir Khan of Rampur), he often expressed, especially while talking about the khayal maestro Amir Khan, the necessity of thumri as a light dessert after a heavy musical item. He himself developed a unique style of light music with a lot of folk colour to overcome his thumriless musical upbringing, away from baijis and nautch girls in the village of Maihar. The Khamaj, Pilu or Bhairavi raags that he had learnt were basically dhrupad based, which he textured by adding folk influences from various provinces and the percussion lilt of the south. The effect was superb, and became the distinguishing feature of his recitals as well as his imaginative scores for films. He extended the horizons of music very much like Faiyaz Khansahab. Music in the twentieth century gained a lot from the way he enhanced the role of rhythmic variations in instrumental music.

The entire Imdadkhani gharana covering four generations of brilliant sitarplaying was instrumental in indirectly privileging the baaj of the sarangi. They copied vocalists like the sarangi and even changed the structure of the sitar to a gandhar pancham to suit this, not only in the super fast taans, but in the five-note complex meend-pulling. The tradition of sarangi-playing in the gharana inspired conversion of vocal patterns; and their sustained effect came to be reflected in the instrumental toḍas which were replaced by khayal taans. In other words, the predominance of the vocal came in through the sarangi which was played by the founder of this gharana and his son Imdad Khan who, with his son Enayat Khan and grandson Vilayat Khan, firmly established this style in the forefront of the sitar world.

In his book *Music and Musicians* Harendrakishore Roy Chowdhury mentions that Imdad Khan played both the sarangi and the jaltarang. The sarangi maestro Ramnarayan once went up to Vilayat Khan after his magnificent Khamaj, and exclaimed, 'apne to sitar ko sarangi bana liya!' What he meant was that the meends were so sustaining, that they had transcended the limitations of a plucked instrument and sounded like the bowing of a sarangi. This compliment from the maestro made Khansahab a bit uneasy, for the past sarangi connection of the grandfather was always played down by the Imdadkhani descendants. This class consciousness in instrumental music is no longer relevant today; but was in the past as strong as the Hindu caste system or the Muslim lineage classification, if not stronger.

Ustad Alauddin Khan made the tabla a more rhythm oriented percussion instrument. Enayat Khan also thought about this in the form of tehai-s on which he worked with Biru Mishra (of Benaras) in Gouripur (now in Bangladesh). He however continued to prefer a non-disturbing theka from his tabla player. 'This is not kathak dance,' the Etawa gharana stalwarts said, 'that we will go together.' Ravi Shankar, in keeping with Baba Alauddin Khansahab's tradition, broke convention and gave unprecedented importance to the tabla player. Ustad Ali Akbar Khan also did it, but in a more limited way. The emerging trends in the USA and Europe also favoured the increased role of tabla and mridangam in recitals of instrumental music. The virtuoso status of the ghatam and mridangam had already been established in the Carnatic music tradition. Ravi Shankar accorded Allahrakha the role of a virtuoso, by introducing tabla solos, and sparkling sawal-jawab interludes in the recital between the sitar and the tabla. The concept of tarparan of the pakhawaj was sought to be revived by the Maihar gharana but was sometimes overdone in their prolonged saath-sangat bouts with the tabla. The tabla maestros would often get equal or greater applause during and after a recital. No knowledge of music was necessary for understanding these bouts. There was excitement and the young generation of music listeners enjoyed the thrill. The majority of listeners were ignorant about raag differences and their melodic brilliance, but everyone understood the language of rhythm. Thus the tabla became very popular with the audience. This elevation of the status of the instrument with maestros like Ustad Ahmedjan Thirakwa, Pandit Samta Prasad to Ustad Allarakha and Ustad Zakir Hussain had been phenomenal between the 1950s and the 1980s, with percussionists becoming objects of popular adulation.

North Indian percussionists as well as their South Indian brothers Raghu Palghatmani Aiyer and followers enjoyed star status. Our music became rhythm oriented after the sixties. This started in the early fifties when Pandit Samta Prasad tipped the sound people to make his sound louder. He was the only tabla player who got a separate applause over and above the joint applause he got with the main performer. Even a traditionalist like Kanai Dutt would often express his admiration at this. What came later in Zakir Hussain's prime time was even more than this. Zakir consistently enriched his training from his father Allarakha with the best he could get from the sister gharanas, particularly Afaque Hussain and Nizamuddin and superimposed on it a progressive version of the brilliant right-left hand sound effect pioneered by the legendary Samta Prasad.

Instead of closing their eyes to listen to the meditative raag alap the audience eagerly looked forward to rhythm entertainment. Music also changed colour and the inevitable conclusion of a recital with fast rhythm display became the norm. Some, like Ustad Vilayat Khan and his riyazi clan, tried to match this with technical brilliance and virtuosity; but in both cases raag melody as well as time honoured authentic raag phrases took a subservient position. Fast dazzling passages are bound to give less importance to complicated phrases and Yaman simplified to a sampooran raag, will be played instead of Kamod or Kedar and Ahir Bhairav more than Bilaskhani Todi. In their quest to reach the masses, rhythm was privileged; melody and melodic creativity suffered. Rhythm consciousness not so strougly present with the veenkar stalwarts fifty years ago was now stronger. There was some gain, but traditional Indian classical music became percussion-heavy and almost went pop.

Some tabla players became so preoccupied with their new found status that they started making trouble on the stage for more sound volume and offstage for equal fees and larger prominence in advertisements and hoardings. This did not work out except in fusion bands. The very popular ones in accompaniment failed to draw people in their solo concerts. Students they had aplenty, but the general melody thirsty Indian music audience would hear and applaud percussion only as a supplement to music. The concept of tabla solos did not work out commercially, with the exception of Ustad Zakir Hussain, who also excelled in East-West fusions. His first fusion album *Shakti and Shakti 2* became very popular. Some harking back towards melody in the nineties kept Bismillah Khan and Vilayat Khan as redolent of the flavours of tradition, but still too little to match the grand combinations of percussion and melody which drew people in thousands in India and abroad.

THE SITAR AND RAVI SHANKAR

If Faiyaz Khansahab had presented Indian music with an enhanced canvas to outshine the dhrupadiyas and khayaliyas of his time in dignity, stature and popularity, Ravi Shankar did the same to outshine his predecessors, whom he could not otherwise match in right hand force and virtuousity. Those who played before his arrival in the sitar world, viz. Imdad Khan, Inayat Khan, Wahid Khan, Mohammad Khan, Mushtaq Ali Khan, all had strong and balanced right hand movements perfectly coordinated with left hand meend, gamak and sapat. Instead of brooding over details of gharanadar techniques in sitar playing, he included whatever was possible to enrich his sitar music format. The Masitkhani gat particularly was given a more enriched look with as much systematic expansion as the preceding alap and joḍ. His compositions in the other taals were played with the ease and spontaneity of teen tal. His musical expressions were also more organized and always edited to perfection. His approach to drut compositions were more like stepping stones to jhala, which he never elongated, for with his hooked kharaj-pancham, he was intelligent enough not to make his drut or fast taans comparable to other open stringed contemporaries. Had he wanted to do this he would have been prevented by the kharaj-pancham in his sitar which even hooked would go out of tune. Nikhil Banerjee could, with his early training under gharanadar sitar players and his fourteen-hours practice, do this, though within a very limited group of raags. An enhancement in canvas, be it in music or art, is bound to affect the level of technical virtuosity possible within a limited range of raags.

Raviji was handicapped by his surbahar oriented sitar, which helped his alap, with one extra base octave in kharaj-pancham, but made his right hand movement more difficult. What he did within these constraints was remarkable and the work of a genius, be it in rhythm variation, taal vocabulary, raag-baḍhat system, saath-sangat excitement or dance lilt. He used hooks to his advantage, to prevent the strong, thick, wavering strings from humming aloud and controlled free movement of the right hand. This only helped him partly and he did what he could with his caged right hand. He used the punctuation of a dancer, and dramatized passages with a brilliant grasp over laya and calculation, which he had already disciplined himself to. This singsong, meandering melody made listeners forget the absence of the strong traditional sitar right hand, or even the continuous left hand meend-work. They welcomed the innovation and creativity, which only the genius of an agile and aware man could offer—with intense practice and musical insight. Ravi Shankar's greatest contribution was in establishing sitar playing as an effective combination of the technique / dexterity and intelligent and effective planning. To him, music output was more important than showing off what long hours of practice was capable of, or even the special training he had received in the mechanics of instrumental music. The brilliant compositions of his guru were used only sparingly. This was also because the long bandishes of the guru which he had learnt meticulously had to be matched by even longer taans made more difficult by his arrested right hand movement and the complicated raags which only he could effectively play even in a country full of gharanadar musicians. His popularity and success can be attributed equally to his training under Baba Alauddin Khan, and his own genius and foresight.

Panditji clearly understood that large gat compositions required elaborate improvisation patterns. It is a pity that the few musicians in India who have had the good luck to inherit or learn them do not understand this. A sixtyfour-beat fast composition would require at least one hundred or more beat lengthy taans to match it. This requires stamina and is often exhausting on the stage where aesthetics and pure raag interpretation have to be matched with the beat tempo—with perfect coordination with the mind and the hand. Vilayat Khan also understood this and mostly played short khayal compositions to match and bring forward his beautiful meend and fret-combined taans in the latter half of his life. Gharana exponents who did not understand this were gradually wiped out of the concert scene, much to their frustration.

THE NIYAMATULLAH KHAN SAROD GHARANA

The Niyamatulla Khan sarod gharana had a huge repertoire of Rezakhani and Ferozekhani compositions set in teental, but has been rendered almost extinct in the absence of capable representatives who can match the high standards of the gharana. This gharana reached its zenith in the beginning of the twentieth century, when his two sons Keramatulla and Kukub (Kaukav) Khan were so popular that the Kolkata business community, with the approval of the then British viceroy, sponsored their performance at the anniversary of Queen Victoria's coronation. One Enayat Ali Khan of the same family also played at the same programme. Enayat Ali was a disciple of Umrao Khan Veenkar. The glory of this gharana survived till Sakhawat Hussain, whose recordings are available on the Internet, but vanished from performance circles after the death of Ishtiaq Ahmed in Delhi. All shudh notes are sometimes played side by side with a Komal Gandhar-based Rezakhani gat. Sakhawat Hussain used to be Enayat Khan's competitor and was a brilliant sarod player, proud of his bandish heritage. Enayat Khan ushered in an era of personal genius winning over tradition.

Their competition went to a personal level when Enayat Khansahab announced his name after the conclusion of a mizrap-played-esraj in Khamaj, as 'Sakhawat ka baap.' Sakhawat's lawyer promptly demanded one lakh rupees in those days as compensation for defamation. This was around 1936 and Imrat Khan had just been born. On the advice of lawyers, Enayat Khansahab immediately changed Imrat's name to Sakhawat and escaped the defamation fine. The name was changed back to the original once again when matters cooled down.

SHORTENING OF TRADITIONAL COMPOSITIONS

One way to escape this heavy burden of large bandishes was to shorten the compositions so that the vistars and fast taans were privileged in comparison. Both Ravi Shankar and Vilayat Khan did this; the former, by playing a shortened version with right hand bolbanis to keep the old world flavour; and the latter by changing the whole movement pattern with left hand prominent vocal composition-parts starting from the ninth or the twelfth beat to make things even easier, after a superfast taan.

I have always been more attached to the playing of Vilayat Khan and Ali Akbar Khan, for their catchy improvised patterns often haunted me in my leisure hours; but given the option of hearing the same musician every day, for ten days for example, I would always opt for Pandit Ravi Shankar. One reason was that one could learn from him every day. He did not brood over self-created beautiful passages but thought about the totality of presentation and offering the raag in its true spirit. Ravi Shankar also tried some sort of standardization in raag interpretation, striking a balance between Ustad Alauddin Khan and Pandit Vishnu Narayan Bhatkhande, for the sake of acceptance by connoisseurs, as well as anyone who knew some basic Indian music. His was a constant effort to reach the masses which Vilayat Khan described as the language of the Tansens and the 'Kan-sens' [lit. 'kan' means 'ear'; meaning the uninitiated, who only hear.]

Mudraki Kanara, for example, was never played or taught by his father, Ali Akbar Khan would recall, but Raviji's inquisitive mind would dig up the raag character from known sources like Birendrakishore Roychaudhuri's collection or even Bhatkhande, and play its standardized version acceptable to all. When he played Sindhura, I remember he did not play his guru's version with two nikhads but the Mushtaq Hussain–Dabir Khan–Radhikamohan Maitra version of only komal nishad with the more prominent dhaivat to keep a distance from the Agra gharana version of Barwa. This intellect and rationality in approach makes Ravi Shankar unique. The addition of a kharaj string had given him a bass octave like the surbahar. The original low bronze pancham string did give the sitar player some space to move beyond jodi—but only by two notes if you did not count the open bronze pancham string, and three if you did. This was too little for complete phrase formation and sitar players preferred to stay within the limit of the jodi Sa, in the fear that the thick pancham itself might be slightly off key. Vilayat Khan thought it to be the source of a disturbing buzz during fast playing and, unable to control it, took it out of the sitar and replaced it with a steel gandhar for chikari enrichment, as well as the tanpura effect of a vocalist. Mushtaq Ali rarely used the bronze or brass pancham he had after the jodi duel.

Ravi Shankar used it with another thicker bronze string on the side, adding not only four more fret notes, but three more meend notes, for the kharaj string had the space to be pulled. This made the string itself, capable of one octave playing as it was further left, and improved meend space compared to the traditional bronze pancham. This string with the bronze pancham added one complete octave of pulling and fret playing with totally different tonal colours. The main string had its own steel tone; the jodi a different sound texture; now the pancham and kharaj gave two more tone timbres to make Ravi Shankar's sitar totally different from existing sitars, and richer in the variety of tonal colours. His elegantly decorated blood-brown sitar with an additional veena-like gourd now had a majestic personality made richer by the beautiful way he used it. The alap would unfold within minutes, with the full raag in view, and move on to a brilliant display of the bass strings—in a manner only Ravi Shankar was capable of—making the sitar a more crisp and clear version of the veena.

STRING ARRANGEMENT IN SITAR AND VEENA

The string setting of this sitar was different from that of the parent veena. If we start from the side of the chikari strings, the first playing string was the kharaj, then come the pancham and jodi and the main string. Being on the other side, the kharaj got maximum space for meend movement. It is opposite in the traditional rudra veena. The kharaj comes last from this side and the first from the other side. In the veena the thickest string occupies the same position as the sitar's main string. Pulling possibilities in the veena was also limited by the shape, length and construction of the frets. The main string of the sitar is now an improved version of a German Klavier steel string and cannot be broken easily even if it is tuned to high tension D and stretched to the fifth note. In the true veenkar tradition, Ravi Shankar, a Senia representative, chose not to make the chikari strings too rich and loud. It was almost nonexistent as the ancient rudra veenas, but loud enough to assist his raag material prominent alap and to get an applause in his straight jump to a fast jhala after a drut gat or joḍ. This jhala, in contrast, sounded even faster for its suddenness and clarity. These thin chikaris, a little louder than the parent rudra veena, gave the main string greater prominence. In sound terminology, the main string was brought forward to advantage and not merged or submerged in the cacophony of other strings. It was amazing how, even when he was eighty, Raviji maintained this jump to the fast jhala after joḍ.

Ustad Vilayat Khan was also intelligent enough to avoid the right hand intricacies of his forefathers. Forcefulness and power which shone in the microphoneless music rooms of yesteryears had the danger of misfiring with sound amplification of the microphone. He saw how the brilliance of Mushtaq Ali Khan's right hand suffered from the earlier double joḍi stringed sitar. Even Mushtaq Ali's uniform balanced strokes appeared monotonous for the constant buzzing of the dual joḍi and lack of sound modulation. Mushtaq Ali was distinctive because of the uniformity of right hand strokes. Such balance can rarely be heard in sitar; but in the microphone era this went against him, because the listener missed tonal variation. The listeners also missed the percussion orientation and effective application which Ravi Shankar very intelligently filled up to his advantage.

Unable to match his father or grandfather in right hand power, Vilayat Khan started research on the possibilities of the left hand playing and achieved the impossible task of incorporating all nuances and melody detail vocalists could offer. His right hand lacked the strength of his ancestors but he made this up by a brilliant sitar tone and together with Ali Akbar Khan developed tonal variation and modulation in Indian instrumental music hitherto heard only in certain special passages of Ustad Enayat Khan and Hafiz Ali.

MUSHTAQ ALI KHAN

Mushtaq Ali Khan was, for a short time after Enayat Khan's death in 1938, the most sought after sitar player in the country. He combined in his music the solid raag base of the Senias with the sweetness of Enayat Khansahab's gharana. Enayat Khansahab had been so impressed by the young Mushtaq Ali's good looks and melodious sitar that he had wanted him as his son-in-law. This did not materialize. Had it been otherwise, there would have been a grand fusion of two famous sitar gharanas, according to Radhikamohan Maitra. This also could have been a disaster. Mushtaq Ali's gharanadar ragdari and Enayat Khan's technique remains the ideal model for aspiring sitar players.

Ustad Mushtaq Ali Khan's father Ashique Ali Khan was a disciple of Barkatulla Khansahab and represented the undiluted Senia sitar playing of western India, kept alive by Amrit Sen, the king of sitar in the pre-Imdad Khan era. For reasons unknown Mushtaq Ali left home while he was still in his teens and took employment in the court of the Maharaja of Darbhanga. Vocalist Anathnath Bose brought him to Kolkata, where he later became a disciple of the sarod maestro Mohammad Ameer Khan. Mohammad Ameer Khan was a moving storehouse of 16-beat teental Reza Khani and Feroze Khani gat compositions, inherited from his father Abdulla Khan, the adopted son of Murad Ali Khan. Radhikamohan Maitra, his favourite disciple, learnt these compositions and perfected them in the purity of Senia raag phrases from Mohammad Dabir Khan for seventeen long years.

In the early 1950s Mushtaq Ali's concerts dwindled, because he refused to compromise, but concentrated on teaching, and trained a number of very good sitar players. He commanded respect in Kolkata, where he stayed till the last day of his life. Nikhil Banerjee was one of his students and in spite of all the training in the Maihar gharana, retained Mushtaq Ali's right hand training till the end. The right hand fingers were spread to their natural maximum in Ra or the outward movement in sitar (in sarod it is the opposite: the outward movement is called Da and the inward movement Ra).

In the 1940s, Mushtaq Ali introduced Ravi Shankar to Kolkata in a concert arranged in Ratan Sarkar's home (house of the famous jeweller M B Sarkar's). Raviji never looked back after this. Mushtaq Ali agreed to play a duet with the little known and struggling Vilayat Khan who played storms of taans to outshine his patron. Mushtaq Ali was non-commercial in approach, but his greatness as a brilliant teacher and uncompromising traditionalist remained till his death. He played a seventeen-fret sitar, an older version of the nineteen-fretted one used now, and stayed away from the stage, except the regular once a month radio broadcast. To him this music was one hundred per cent tradition and he did not care for the excitement the new audience wanted. His chosen raag flowered within moments of commencement of playing—with a copybook precision that never faltered at old age—and the smoothness and spontaneity remained intact.

THE SITAR TODAY

The mid-twentieth century saw two transformations in the sitar: one was the surbahar-sitar mix in Ravi Shankar's sitar; the other was the single jodi gandhar-pancham Vilayat Khani sitar as it is called today. Ravi Shankar's was the traditional bara sitar of yore minus one of the jodi pair, plus a thick bronze sharaj or coloquial kharaj tuned to Sa, an octave lower than the jodi Sa. This was in line with the one designed to copy the veena in the Senia gharana for students outside the family. Ustad Alauddin Khan went to Yusuf Ali Khan, the sitar player / sitar maker of Lucknow and asked him to make a sitar similar to the bara sitar or what was known as the veena substitute a hundred years ago, designed for non-family shagirds, of the descendants of Mian Tansen. This sitar was much bigger than the one used for Sufi music and folk music, and slightly bigger than the usual sitar played by Senia sitar players. It had two gourds; one closed and the upper one open, giving a natural monitor to the musician; and the dand or neck slightly thicker for more meend range.

The surbahar, as we know it today after it changed the gourd to a tortoise shaped one, is an enlarged version of the bara sitar. The Imdadkhani clan claims this to be their contribution as well as the putting in of tarafs. The enlarged version of the Senia bara sitar with a larger tortoise shaped gourd may have been designed by Imdad Khan, but not the bara sitar itself. The concept is definitely Senia and probably the brain child of Umrao Khan, a descendant of Tansen. Imdad Khan developed it. Even then, the enlarged tortoise shaped version is a brilliant development, and the Imdadkhani gharana should be proud of being responsible for this, for never before in the history of world music has a full octave seven-note meend been pulled from one note, in a plucked instrument. Sahajad Mohammad from whom Imdad learnt, must have been playing the veena copy capable of a maximum of four-note meends. This— instead of humming the half-truth that surbahar owes its origin to the Etawa gharana—should have been highlighted. The meend range enhanced, modified kachva surbahar with tarafs and chikaris taken from the sarangi, is perhaps Imdad Khan and his Etawa gharana's most significant contribution to instrumental music.

ALAUDDIN KHAN

Ustad Alauddin Khan was a great reviver. He revived the bara sitar, and enhanced the span of alap in sitar. He also enhanced the canvas of gath elaboration by reviving in a new form the sath and ladguthao mentioned in the twelve parts of instrumental music playing. He also revived raags, infusing them with rare innovativeness and creativity. His knowledge was vast. His Hemant and Hem Behag are probably the most played and accepted among recent creations and revivals. In Hemant, the shudh Basant teevra madhyam and komal rekhav climbed up half a note each to become shudh rekhav and pancham—giving any instrumentalist who chose to play this raag, full scope for alap as well as fast taan expansion. In Hem Behag, the original bilaval ang Behag played even a hundred years ago, where teevra madhyam was rarely used, was maintained, and the emphasis shifted to shudh madhyam. Probably both these raags, especially the latter one, was invested its present aesthethic structure by making some deviations from the original form, by Ustad Ali Akbar Khan. These raags have survived nearly sixty years. Others tried this, but at the most they managed to give a concert or two themselves. No one else willingly followed.

USTAD IMDAD KHAN

The modern sitar is indebted to Imdad Khan for its present form, both in structure and technique of playing. Born in Etawa, he was the son of Sahabdat Khan, who was born to a Rajput and converted to Islam when his paternal aunt got married to one of the Haddu-Hassu Khan brothers. Jitendramohan Sengupta mentions Sahabdat as Haddu Khan's 'shyalak-putra' [son of Haddu Khan's brother-in-law]. The sarangi, the most common and popular musical instrument of the Rajputs, was Sahabdat's oldest companion. It was both the connecting link to the Khan household and also the reason why the connection was prolonged and sustained. Sahabdat Khan was a comparatively unknown khayaliya, who played the sitar, the sarangi and the jaltarang, and was happy to remain active in research and enrichment within the Haddu-Hassu household. His hard working and talented son Imdad Khan heard exquisite music from his birth and could also play the three instruments his father had taught him. He imbibed whatever he could from sitar, khayal, and sarangi, and blended them effectively in a style of playing, which become famous as the Imdadkhani sitar baaj. He also mastered the jaltarang, and gained command over rhythm and laya—a rare acievement in those days. Most of the Senia greats who preceeded him, were so immersed in raag melody that laya got little importance. His first love remained the sitar; and with his fourteen hours of daily practice soon became famous as one who could do anything with the sitar at a speed unimaginable by his contemporaries or predecessors.

He already had a vocal grooming in khayal, and not a veena background, as was usual in those days. He played the sarangi and jaltarang or water xylophone in addition. It was with the enormous reproductive power of this instrument that young Sahab could delve into the vocal intricacies of the Gwalior gharana and it was the sarangi that helped him to translate vocal idioms into sitar, his next love, thereby laying the foundation of the khayal-gayaki sitar style. The shrutidhar sarangi-jaltarang-sitar player's music would not have been accepted by the intelligensia as pedigreed, gharanadar music, had it not been for the finishing touch of the Senia sitar stalwart Sahajad Mohammad Khan. The guru's role in the ideal instrumental music training is to make the student achieve control over the instrument and its technique by hours of palta or permutation-combination practice. When this preparation base is satisfactorily completed, the guru goes forward with composition and elaboration training. In Imdad's case this was already accomplished in the first phase of his life through his father, as well as his exposure to stalwarts connected to Haddu-Hassu and Bande Ali Khan veenkar. With this solid training, he could absorb the essence of Sahajad Mohammad's playing easily and effectively—perhaps much more effectively than the Senia shagirds, who were technically no match for Imdad Khan.

This sarangi connection has however been played down by his descendants. This was probably because in those days, sarangi was said to be the lowest in the hierarchy of musical instruments. In fact it goes to the credit of Imdad Khan that he was a maestro in three instruments, viz. the sitar, the sarangi, and the jaltarang. This, in no way diminishes his greatness for his sarangi connection led to his virtuosity in sitar. His roots in the famous Gwalior school and his logical transference of the intricate vocal patterns, via the sarangi into the sitar is, to me, the greatest achievement in instrumental music in the last two centuries.

The ancestral sarangi connection is further proved by the fact that Ustad Amir Khan was chosen as groom for Enayat Khan's and Bashiran-bibi's second daughter, Sarifan-bibi. Amir Khan's father Sameer Khan was a sarangi player of Indore. Under normal circumstances an arranged marriage in those caste-conscious times could not have taken place with a court musician's daughter unless the musician himself had sarangi connections. The Muslim community in those days was even more class conscious than conservative brahmans. The normal division into Sayed claiming Arabian lineage, Shaikh, Pathan, Moghul, conversion from Rajputs, conversion from artisans, and conversion from untouchables have been rigorously followed in the arranged marriages of this community. Dumont has rightly pointed out that the rigidity and conservatism of this class system based on lineage often outdid the neighbouring caste Hindus in practice. All abuses were also decorated with the father brought in (in the bachcha series) as much as the class-conscious British did in those times.

The sarangi player Mamman Khan was Imdad Khan's leading sarangi student, proving that while dominating the sitar scene he still maintained his sarangi connection and adored its musical possibilities. In his formative years Imdad Khan practised up to fourteen hours a day to achieve what had not yet been achieved in this instrument, a one-stroke-one-note format, to bring out what

vocal music and sarangi could. The idea of taraf strings to resonate
the upper meend and fret playing may have also been borrowed
from the sarangi. The sitar therefore should not only be indebted
to the mother veena but also to the brother sarangi for its unparalleled
tonal variety, sustenance of meend, and vocal colour. His left leg
was damaged permanently due to long hours of practice, seated in
that half-lotus posture. His primary attention was the sitar and the
surbahar; and though he was influenced by Nirmal Shah veenkar
(of direct Senia lineage), guru of mentor and senior relative Bande
Ali Khan, he did not distract himself with the complexities of
raagdari or raag training in the beginning of his sitar career. Instead
of following the path of the veena as was usual in those days, he
gave the sitar and surbahar a personality of their own which would
overtake the mother instrument rudra veena within the next half a
century, both in instrumental capacity and appeal, even if we refrain
from speaking about popularity.

One has to admit that this was possible because the bow instrument
insight gave him the vision to sustain notes. This he did by making
the instrument and the strings stronger, the dand of the sitar and
surbahar and its frets wider and meend technique more sustainable.
It is quite possible that vocal ornamentation details were preserved
in the sarangi and then transferred to sitar in more detail than a
direct transfer. Instrument to instrument transfer is always more
precise and accurate.

A part of the toḍas which involved more than one stroke on a
single note were translated into one-stroke-one-note khayal taans,
a rarity in those days. He played both toḍa and taan with equal
skill and the force of his right hand and their electrifying effect
kept the knowledgeable veena-groomed sitar players at bay. His
fast taans and robust right hand toḍas in the sitar were designed to
match Haddu-Hassu Khan's forceful singing as it were; and

remained his forte till the next generation started changing them to one-stroke-one-note taans. For example gg mm or gggg mmmm became gradually gm (g is 'ga', and m is 'ma' in the middle octave).

THE SITAR AND VILAYAT KHAN

Vilayat Khan also worked on the tone of the sitar. With the help of Hiren Roy, the wonderful sitar maker of Kolkata, he omitted one of the two joḍis and replaced this with the steel gandhar. I do not remember his sitar having any bronze pancham. This made the tone crisp, the meends wider, and the taans crystal clear with no joḍi disturbance. He had learnt that joḍi disturbance could throttle even the brilliance of Mushtaq Ali's balanced right hand and took out one of them, to increase its distance from the main string. This freed the right hand from space impairment. He also enhanced the pitch of the sitar from C which was usual then, to C-sharp, in the 1950s, and gave the main string a sonorous tone. No one could match this. To all sitar players irrespective of gharana, the tone of Vilayat Khan's sitar remained a dream. They all increased their pitch to C sharp and eventually to D. All this was done by the mid-1950s. Nikhil Banerjee was quick to follow. The Maihar clan also followed their beloved Nikhil-da, and indirectly followed Vilayat Khan in tone, meend and whatever they could do in sapat taans.

The sitar, which had already developed an individual personality, distinct from the veena in the hands of Enayat Khan and Imdad Khan—Vilayat Khan's father and grandfather respectively—now distanced itself even further. With its five-note meend, vigorous fast gamaks, and sapats, and their enhanced force and dramatic conclusions, the sitar became a separate instrument, as if made for this fast music. It developed a character diametrically opposite to what the veena stood for. This was achieved under Vilayat Khan, the only sitar player who went in the opposite direction of Ravi Shankar's bara sitar.

THE CHANGING COURSE OF INDIAN CLASSICAL MUSIC

Indian music had never remained static. It has always changed with time. The form of a raag has been maintained in its overall picture, but never in the European way of notation with its punctuation, tempo, and detail intact. Rapport with the audience has always been essential for the Indian musician, often in the form of direct appreciation and applause in the middle of a concert. The court musician had to keep his patrons—the kings and courtiers—satisfied for his bread came from there. The concert musician of the twentieth century needed to satisfy a larger audience and the percussionist was brought forward to advantage perhaps without realizing that a rather complicated problem was being created, which in the not so distant future would devour a good part of the melody that was supposed to be embellished.

The entertainment demanded by an eighteenth century musician-king could in no way compare with the demands of the twentieth century audience. In some princely states, where the king himself was a knowledgeable musician, alap and slow passages developed. The entire research of the musician was confined to the gradual progression of note patterns, linked to each other with smoothness and spontaneity—silsila without jerks was the aim. Thus the veenkar style of the Senias, the descendants of Tansen (the legendary sixteenth century court musician of Akbar the great) flourished. Early twentieth century landlords and nouveau riche traders required brighter and faster entertainment, as most of them did not have any pedigree in music, and appreciated only what was light, simple, sensuous and fast.

The Patiala-Punjab gharana came into prominence with their colourful, ornamentation-heavy thumris. The importance of the theory of raags went to the background. This was in the beginning. Later, Bhatkhande's monumental work aimed at preservation and standardization of raag patterns, with the now involved middle class intelligentsia in Maharashtra and Bengal, reopened a probe into authentic, and standardized raag patterns and phrases. This coincided with political awareness, the nationalist movement, and the pride of having a grand musical heritage. Records, archives, and radio broadcasts brought about some raag awareness among the majority of listeners who liked music but had never had the opportunity of any formal training in music. Thus basic raags like Yaman and Bhairav and their standardized versions were no longer unknown to the regular listener. The sitar audience wanted fun and excitement in music recitals. They demanded speed, skill, and percussion-heavy music. Melody receded to the background and raag composition both in vocals and sitar.

In the past, it was the composition that guided the improvisation, not letting it go wild, and providing it with the security of a nest to return to. This nest would automatically control the line or angle of baḍhat or expansion even if there is a tendency to slip out of the raag track and lose way. These beautiful compositions with their built-in raag elaboration were either not sung or played, or unnecessarily shortened as the century proceeded. This happened more in the sitar tradition-rich Bengal than vocal tradition-rich Maharashtra, where it was difficult to ignore the poetry–music amalgam. Authentic pure music survived in different proportions in different parts of the country. The best atmosphere for our music still lives on in the music circles, and small baithaks all the way from Mumbai and Pune up to Bangalore.

Even at the beginning of the twentieth century the audience was closed in a microphoneless music room. The priority was quest for authenticity. When the young Imdad Khan played a two hour concert with breathtaking taans and brilliant chikari work, the old and feeble Amrit Sen played a Darbari Kanara alap for eight minutes and stopped. Imdad Khan stood up with folded hands and asked, 'Will you exchange your eight minutes with my two hours?' 'No,' Amrit Sen replied, 'that's not possible; you live on with your power, skill and virtuosity—and I, with my authenticity, peace and simplicity.' The inherited ancient cannot be exchanged for something achieved personally by hard labour. This victory of melody, raag training, aesthethic beauty and feeling over technical mastery and speed; and its acknowledgement started to dwindle as the century progressed, for Veer and Shringar rasa took over Karun and Bhakti rasa in a world where finesse and delicacy had started fading out.

There was also an urge to escape from the mechanics of regimented music. This is evident in the creation of new gharanas. Alauddin Khan was different from Rampur, so was Hafiz Ali and Mushtaq Hussain; so we now had three styles instead of one, viz. Maihar, Gwalior and Sahaswan. All these three greats learned from Wazir Khan. Faiyaz Khan differed from Zohra Bai, Bade Ghulam Ali was too mellow for Patiala and Ali Akbar Khan too sweet for the Khandarbani Maihar Gharana as developed by Baba Alauddin. Each gharana now had in its brilliant exponents such wealth of ideas for its improvement and expansion, that the root gharana was sometimes completely overshadowed by individual genius. Personality now dominated over lineage.

Raag detail if carried too far poses the danger of throttling the creative urge of a romantic musician. Some gharana stalwarts in Agra, Atrauli and Jaipur insisted on a verbatim reproduction of the lines taught. The Dagar gharana did the same. Punjab also did not lag behind, insisting on the mouth being opened wide during singing, making the scene comical especially for women. Our music is essentially personal, though on a gharana guru-vidya base; else gharanas would not have multiplied so effectively and easily. Paradoxically however, gharanas bear in their most intelligent students the kernel of their gradual destruction.

The same formula even in orthodox gharanadar teaching can only be applied to all for the first three years. After this it should be varied at least in degree according to the capability and personality of the individual student. Interplay of alap or fast taans and the note combinations required, differs from person to person and depends on subjective vocal capacity. Regimentation of all in one pattern may lead to disaster. Prasun Banerjee and Bhishmadev Chattopadhyay were both God's gifts to Bengal. Their association with Patiala and Agra gharanas in the mature stages of their career did not yield good results. In life there is a natural flow and an artificial one. One should always opt for the former, for in all forms of expression—art, music, or literature—the formation of a structure demands a smooth course without the jolts and jerks, which are inevitable, if artificially superimposed.

Abdul Karim Khan emerged straight from heaven as it were, and taught musicians and listeners what natural expression was. Born in 1874, he did not live long, but within a span of twenty years in the beginning of the century gave people a glimpse of heavenly music. Whether he sang Bhairavi or Jogia, Bhimpalasi or Jhinjhoti, he surpassed grammar and attracted anybody who knew how to laugh and cry. In Maharashtra his style was kept alive in Hirabai Barodekar, Gangubai Hangal, Bhimsen Joshi, and dozens of others. The Kirana style was natural, liberal, and romantic, and freed the musicians from the chains of rigidity and reactionary conservatism. A straightforward link was established between the performer's feeling and expression. The influence of the sarangi with its folk roots may have given the style a feeling of the soil with its sorrow and happiness to make it more communicative.

Alladiya Khan was yet another master who influenced music with his inimitable style. He was born in 1859 and lived till 1946. At the turn of the century he was an active performer, but soon

concentrated on teaching students. As a teacher he kept alive the
Jaipur style, but probably put this in his own mould, for nowhere in
India do we find this type of medium paced bandishi composition
based singing. As a court musician in Kolhapur he was loved and
admired. He wore the dhoti unlike other Muslim musicians and
was accepted by the Maharashtrians as their own. A statue of
Khansahab has been erected in the heart of Kolhapur and shows
how much the people there loved him. Although his roots were
dhrupads, he employed a slightly faster pace than one hears in the
Rampur Senia style. The feeling is more, perhaps because the
very slow nom-tom alap is absent. As we have already discussed
earlier, the reduction in the tempo and pace of alap was a product
of an interaction between the veenkars and dhrupadiyas for mutual
enrichment. This probably started around the mid-nineteenth
century. Alladiya Khansahab, though born later, was probably a
product of the pre-nom-tom era, and followed that pace of dhrupad
as was sung before his time. His khayal is as bandish based as
dhrupad and revolves around the mokam or bandish with only short
punctuations. The phrases sometimes never do anything which is
not present in the bandish in the true spirit and form of authentic
dhrupad elaboration. The vistar revolves around the song like a
bird around his nest and never rises high enough to lose track.

Bandish-based singing can never be very slow. To have a form
with language, it has to maintain a pace where the words are
recognizable—not as slow as nom-tom alap [in which the original
auspicious phrase 'ananta Hari om' has tonal patterns superimposed
on it to unfold the selected raag in slow, medium and fast tempo
without employing song-text and beat], so that melody receives
cent per cent attention of the performer, and is not divided between
melody and lyric. The patron-nawab is also happy and not disturbed
by frequent references to the avatar of Vishnu. The Jaipur-Atrauli
style of counting the beats by touching the fingers while singing

also reminds me of Amarnath Bhattacharya of Entally, a disciple of the typical Bengal school of Dhrupad led by Aghornath Chakravarty who did the same. Aghor-babu was a contemporary of Alauddin Khan's first guru Nulo Gopal. Amarnath-babu wobbled his way to the stage, when I saw him last at the Canal Street residence of music lover Adrijanath Mukherjee. But the moment he sang the first line of his dhrupad 'Madhusudana . . .'—the tremor vanished and his voice was steady and the notes pure. Shauqat Ali Khan, my tabla guru who accompanied him on the pakhawaj, observed, 'The musician tremors, but the voice and the laya are as solid as rock. My salute to his guru for the disciplined training he gave him.' The Dhrupad school of Bengal was as composition-based as Alladiya Khan's dhrupad-based khayals. Both were representative of a style which preceded the slow nom-tom style of the Dagars; always weaving around musical patterns prompted by the composition with its four parts—asthayi, antara, sanchari and abhog.

The pre-nom-tom bandish-baḍhat days probably started ending with some exceptions after the time of veenkar Bande Ali Khan. The veenkar families saw some new entrants by marriage, viz. Haddu Khan and Bairam Khan Dagar. Khayal, dhrupad and veena all interacted to create the slow meditative nom-tom alap as well as the not too meditative fast joḍ at khayal fast taan speed, and veena jhala speed, which the late Moinuddin Dagar sang with his fingers moving in the instrumental jhala way while singing.

Ustad Hafiz Ali Khan's singing sarod also wove patterns around dhrupad compositions in the pre-nom-tom raag-heavy style, though at a much slower tempo than the Jaipur-Atrauli gharana of Alladiya Khan. This was probably because of Wazir Khan's veena-baaj influence. The Rampur Seni's dhrupads were more prominent, slower, and more elaborate. One song was enough to elaborate all the prominent elements of the raag concerned. It is a pity that this style has no dhrupad singers today. The late B V Keshkar used to hail Hafiz Ali Khan as the best dhrupad singer he had heard. If this compliment is being given to one, who was basically an instrumentalist, one can imagine the extent of dhrupad talim base in the Rampur-Senia gharana as also the elaborate training of Ganeshiprasad Chaturvedi.

Alladiya Khansahab's training as evident in the singing of Kesarbai Kerkar, Mogubai Khurdikar or Nivrittibua Sarnaik also revolves around the composition, and is deeply imbedded in talim. Talim is not just training as in modern institutions. Here the guru makes sure that the pupil can reproduce what he has taught him, in the same succession, and maintaining the same flavour. The pace can vary a little but not the content. Nivrittibuaji's pace was slightly slower than Mallikarjun Mansur's who had learnt from Alladiya Khan's son Manji Khan. This was perhaps the influence of Sawai Gandharva. Kesarbai was also a bit fast in pace from the beginning and more ornamented. The common factor was the pauseless weaving of raag patterns as far as a single breath could permit. Kishori Amonkar not only sang brilliantly like a nightingale but understood the audience. Her feeling and intelligent editing of talim cast a spell on the audience whenever she was in the mood. She understood well, that this music form, in order to remain evergreen had to be presented in a new bottle. In her days Kesarbai's presentation was novel and this had overshadowed Kishori's mother Mogubai, also a disciple of Alladiya Khan. Kishori was determined not to make the same mistake.

In Maharashtra, khayal and natyasangeet alike were influenced by two gharanas: Abdul Karim's Kirana and Alladiya Khan's Jaipur-Atrauli. The aftab-e-mausiqi somehow could not make much headway here. Concerts he excelled in, but the music influence remained confined to a dozen competent students, or so, and some relatives within the four walls of the Walia tank Agra gharana household. His majestic music combined with his royal temperament which had helped so many musicians of other gharanas including Gangubai Hangal, Ravi Shankar and Ali Akbar Khan, however kept him as a king, and *aftab* till the last days of his life.

TAANS AND TODAS

Under the influence of khayal, taan has come to mean one-note-one-stroke at a fast pace. In earlier times any musical pattern would be known as 'taan.' It was common for veenkars and dhrupadiyas to talk about 'alap ke taaney.' Todas mean more than one stroke in single note or a combination of single, double and four strokes in one note made into patterns played with percussion accompaniment, or without, at the tail end of alap and jod, as the pace of the music is enhanced to a particular speed level.

These phrases in todas were woven in rhythmic patterns for variety, borrowed from the pakhawaj and enriched by traditional percussion patterns with their researched in-rhythm punctuations. Taans in those days could mean alap taans or phrases bringing out the character of a raag. Today the meaning has changed and one always associates taans with one-stroke-one-note fast movements. Borrowed from khayal in vocal music and sarangi in instrumental music, it did not exist in this speed in the earlier instruments like the veena, sursringar and sur-rabab. Possibly some of it was played at a slower speed in tar-paran, but never in the one-note-one-stroke pattern at a pace higher in speed than madh-jod.

HIERARCHY IN MUSIC

The Hindu religion had always shunned dead skins and those who work with them. Probably this began with ayurvedic caution to prevent infection. Later to enforce this, those who worked with them were made untouchable lower castes. The caste Hindus clung to this in the name of tradition; the Muslim brethren followed this quite rigidly too, though they chose to be different in all other matters.This may also be because even after conversion, they could not get rid of the past ideas ingrained in the family tradition, or maybe this was also the same wine in the bottle of a different religion faced with similar environmental hazards of the tropical subcontinent.

Instruments that used skin components were kept aside in the past for the casteless, not to be played by either caste Hindus or class-conscious Muslims. Brahmans who dared to break rules in Varanasi for example were thrown out of the locality marked for brahmans; took shelter in Kabir Chawra, and started living within their own rebellious, music-practising community. These two instruments also comprised the primary string and percussion support for songs and dances at the kothas of the tawaifs. Hence the stigma attached to the tawaifs also percolated to the tabla and the sarangi, which were considered 'low' in the hierarchy of musical instruments.

Sarangi taans were however as much applauded as fast tabla playing with the Imdadkhani jhala. The veenkar style of the disciples and descendants of Tansen were already overshadowed by the loud, forceful and clear technical power of Imdad Khan. What was most important was that the sitar—till then subservient to the veena—acquired a distinctive personality and showed the potential to dislodge the rudra veena from its regal status, at least in mass following and popularity. It should be noted however, that the trend of reducing raag vocabulary had already begun, and Imdad Khan survived honourably by not playing more than a dozen raags in his life. Reminiscing on the veenkars and sur-rabab and sursringar players, the elderly lamented, 'woh saaz bhi nahi hai woh awaz bhi nahi' ['Neither the ornamentation, nor the sound remains'].

Ustad Imdad Khan was a symbol of hard work and rigorous practice not raagdari. He was a selfmade and highly innovative sitar player, who brought the chikari strings of the sitar to the forefront. He kept the audience spellbound by intricate thok jhala in addition to lengthy meends, fast gamaks and sapats. In thok jhala, the chikari is used in reverse and combines with even more powerful main string strokes. The phrases moved like waves and continuity combined with a very high technical command and aesthetic sense.

SURBAHAR, SITAR, SARANGI

Imdad Khan designed and played a bigger bara sitar called surbahar with a large tortoise-shaped gourd and put prominent taraf strings in both sitar and surbahar. Some are of the opinion that he was the person who pioneered the addition of taraf strings for resonance to outshine the veena. The interesting question that emerges is whether the tarafs were taken from the sarangi, and did the bow sustenance inspire the long meends which outshone the mother instrument, the rudra veena. If so, why play down this brilliant instrument which has in the past and still continues to colour the sitar and surbahar, irrespective of gharana? Even sarod players of the post-Ali Akbar Khan era copy this, leaving their jaba-heavy toda work for academic researchers.

Imdad Khan also initiated sapat taans or taans without pause in sitar and added a new dimension to jhala, where he used the right hand index finger mijrap and the left hand finger meend pulling to create waves of melody in a complete format never presented before. The Senia sitars recorded in those times, including Amrit Sen's disciple Barkatulla Khan's, seemed a little barren, though beautiful. The absence of a powerful jhala from a prominent chikari and the resonance of strings at a geometrically lower level called tarafs were made up by Imdad Khan in collaboration with the sitar makers of Chitpur in north Kolkata.

PERFECTION AND ENHANCEMENT OF STYLE: USTAD ENAYAT KHAN

Imdad Khan's son Enayat Khan took this to even greater heights and with the help of Kanailal, the legendary sitar maker of old Kolkata, made the sitar base even more solid. Brought to Gouripur in Mymensingh district (now in Bangladesh) by Raja Brajendrakishore Roychaudhuri on a salary of two hundred rupees, he taught a number of people apart from Kumar Birendrakishore who learnt for three years and then opted for the parent veena under the octogenarian Mohammad Ali, the last descendant of Mian Tansen, from the son's side. Vilayat Khan, who was as witty as Enayat Khansahab, used to say, 'Khoka Maharaj, why do you always run after the old man (meaning Mohammad Ali) and his slow music? You are young now and should learn the bright music that sitar offers!' Birendrakishore, in his teens, had already got a taste of the spirituality of true Senia alap and was not to be distracted by lighter or brighter forms. Later, he enriched his Senia talim with elaborate lessons from Alauddin Khan, Hafiz Ali Khan, Mohammad Dabir Khan and khayal singers like Mehdi Hussain Khan of Rampur (whose daughter was married to the tabla maestro Keramatulla Khan and is the mother of Sabir who, apart from being a good tabla player has a beautiful voice for lighter music forms). Even with his three year talim Birendrakishore's sitar gave a glimpse of the true Imdadkhani-Enayatkhani baaj within seconds.

One day I asked Vilayat Khansahab why this is not so prominent in other students of Enayat Khan. Vilayat Khan replied that the salary givers' son's lessons are bound to be more authentic. To me this was a very logical and practical answer. My guru Birendrakishore, fully immersed as he was in Senia talim, firmly believed that Enayat Khan was the best sitar performer. He played a handful of raags but never failed. He recalled taking Enayat Khan to Varanasi (Kashi), where in the presence of Kashi Naresh (the king of Kashi) he charmed listeners and wiped out whatever lingered after India's best musicians gave their best. He played Behag and two famous singer-baijis Rasoolan and Kasoolan would not stop weeping after his alap and had to be taken out of the mehfil to be able to start the gaths with tabla. Enayat Khan's strongest point was the maintenance of raag flavour even when he took rebellious liberties. His Dha-ni-Sa Re-ga in Bageshree does not harm the raag flavour nor does his touch of komal gandhar in Bhopali affect continuity, for these are done after the raag flavour is firmly established. The jaltarang talim is evident at the tail end of Rezakhani, just before the beginning of the vigorous pre-jhala toḍa.

Enayat Khansahab's other students included Bipin Das who displayed so much talent that he was allowed to quit his job in the Gouripur kitchen with full pay, to play sitar. He is known as Bipin Ustad who taught a host of disciples in Bangladesh and popularized the Imdadkhani sitar baaj there. His other students were Jyotishchandra Chowdhury and another Birendrakishore of Ramgopalpur. With the Gouripur household living more in Kolkata, Khansahab also rented a small house in Rajabazar not far away from the centre of the city. Here he regularly taught a host of students including Jitendramohan Sengupta, Bimalakanto Roy Chowdhury, Manoranjan Mukherjee, John Gomes, Biren Mitra, Amiyakanti Bhattacharjee and Renuka Saha.

An excellent teacher who had systematized his father's experiments, the ustad paved the way for the city musicians to outshine their paschimi colleagues. Till then the Senia sitar of western India, known as 'Pachao ke sitar', was the most accepted style. It followed their ancestral Masitkhani baaj. Enayat not only decorated this simple baaj with khayal ornamentations and changed its impact, but also created a new form of slow-paced compositions popularly known as Enayatkhani or Imdadkhani. These often started

from the first beat or *sum*. His student Renuka Saha was the first
female performing sitar player together with Shova Kundu. Biren
Mitra's sitar (made by Kanailal) has been played by Vilayat Khan
till his death the other day, and was recognized as the ultimate in
sitar tone. John Gomes taught Nikhil Banerjee and technically
equipped him enough to understand and retain in future, the
intricacies of the gayaki ang, especially the khayal gayaki of Ustad
Amir Khan.

It was in this city that Enayat Khan made his beautiful 78 rpm sitar
recordings which included the Bageshree rendition described earlier,
which in overall flavour kept the raag on track thanks to the sheer
genius of the ustad. Notations do not make or break raags. The
phrases before and after create the raag atmosphere. The base
and flavour already created, artistic liberty sometimes going out of
the framework, merely enhance the beauty of this created base.
This fun of going out of the raag framework was Vilayat Khan's
forte, but unlike his father he did not proudly say that the 'achanak
komal gandhar' in his favourite Bhopali brought him gold medals
in dozens. Ustad Enayat Khan's raag flavour was so strong that
while he got away with a Ni-Sa-Re-Ga-ma-Ga-Re-Sa fast taan in
the conservative Behag, the son could not.

Ustad Enayat Khan dominated the classical instrumental music
scene till his early death in 1938. He created a new type of slow
paced gath, starting from *sum* instead of the usual twelfth beat,
decorating it at each point with khayal ornamentations and tabla
peshkar lilt. These are remembered as Enayatkhani or Imdadkhani.
Together with Biru Mishra the Varanasi tabla player, he introduced
the tabla ang in sitar and developed it. This tabla ang was further
enhanced and taken to great heights by Pandit Ravi Shankar.

Ravi Shankar was so enamoured by Enayat Khan's sitar that he
wanted to learn from him. This was probably the influence of the

late Amiyakanti, a friend of Shankar, whose brilliant right hand toḍas and mizrap work had attracted attention in the All India Music Conference in Allahabad. Unfortunately his string broke in the middle of the concert and he failed to get the gold medal. His musical career did not take off after this but those who knew him admired him for his brilliant right hand mizrap work. A bout of typhoid prevented Shankar from starting sitar lessons under Enayat Khan, and when he recovered, the Ustad had tragically passed away.

Notation of sitar compositions and fixed taans becoming bigger and bigger was Enayat Khan's style of functioning to systematize what Imdad Khan had collected and played. This he successfully did with the help of Gyanadakanta Lahiri and Suresh Chakravarty, both of Mymensingh, and experts in notation writing. Jitendramohon Sengupta was also commissioned to do this when Khansahab was in Rajabazar, Kolkata. Khansahab was paid two hundred rupees to guide and help twice a week. According to Jiten-babu, Bashiran-bibi, Enayat Khan's wife, prevented her husband from teaching him, as Vilayat had already been born. Raja Brojendrakishore found this solution, so that Khansahab, who was basically a very good man, could continue with the musical training with Jiten-babu, even in the face of domestic pressure.

The khayal gayaki perfected by Vilayat Khan had already begun in Imdad Khan's formative period in the Haddu-Hassu household; with paired notes on the sitar gradually transformed into the one-stroke-one-note sapat taans. Some fast toḍas were already transformed into sapat taans with lightning effect which only young Imdad's daily three-candle practice could give. In those days of thick candles and lanterns, a one-candle practice meant a little more than four hours till its last flicker. This was maintained and systematized by Enayat Khan, who added to it a sublime meditative flavour with a perfected Senia style alap in the surbahar.

Besides his father, Imdad Khan mentions the influence of Bande Ali Khan, Rajab Ali Khan and Shahajad Mohammad Khan. The last mentioned according to Pandit Bhatkhande gave his sitar and surbahar a meaningful identity in the classical music world of India. Otherwise, he would have been disposed of as an extremely talented maverick. Enayat Khan told Birendrakishore that he inherited two gharanas, namely his father's ancestral Etawa, and Senia of Sahajad Mohammad. In surbahar, he played alap in the Senia style; in sitar he played Etawa style, purified and corrected in line with the Senia model handed down by his father.

With the help of Kanailal, Enayat Khan made the instrument more robust. This he did, first by ordering a thicker gourd, and then insisting on a thick tabli to match it. The tabli is the front portion of a sitar or surbahar which is glued to the gourd. The white bridge over which the strings are placed in the Indian lute style is fixed on the appropriate position on the tabli. Going over a bridge is typical of the Indian ancient lute. This is why some believe that the veena travelled with the gypsies to Iran and later developed into cither. In Arabia it developed into their khitara. In Spain it became the guitar. In all these instruments the strings go over a bridge and then spread over the entire length of the instrument. Western musicologists do not share this view. They consider the Arabic lute as the father of these instruments and definitely the most ancient.

If the position of the bridge is wrong, the frets in a sitar will be totally out of tune. While putting the bridge, one has to play on the frets, and the accuracy of notes would show whether the position is correct or near correct. The string position over the bridge and its correlation would make clear faults, if any, and help to put the bridge straight. The final test would be to tune the instrument and pull meends and also play staccato on the frets. In an incorrect position, the bridge will move horizontally to find its correct place. Once in its correct position, it would not need anything to stick it into the tabli. Usually a little bit of polish solution is used to cover gaps between the bridge and the tabli to ensure that even when pushed by string movements, the bridge does not shiver. If properly levelled and in correct position, the bridge will not move even without the drop of liquid polish put between the tabli and the bridge. The vertical position will be correct if the fret position is correct and in tune.

For maximum resonance and sustenance of the tone of the sitar, the thickness of the tabli has to be matched with the natural thickness of the gourd before starting the sitar making and assembly work. This is a tough job which can only be done to perfection by a good sitar maker. Khansahab put stronger deer horn plates (now made even stronger with fibre glass ones), and wider metal frets for more meend range, over which his thicker metal strings (number 1 steel was replaced by number 2 and later number 3) could run to the now stronger tuning pegs. The sitar and surbahar which we have inherited are much stronger versions of the sitar played three hundred years ago and the credit for this change goes to Imdad Khan and his son Enayat.

The stronger instrument also achieved a more improved range. Whereas the earlier surbahar (made to copy the veena) did not have more than three and a half note or at the most four note meend capacity, Imdad Khan's descendants could pull up to seven notes from Sa to Ni in this new stronger surbahar and Sa to Pa in the remade sitar. This transformation was necessary because this instrument was made to copy khayal and sarangi in addition to the slow movements of the rudra veena. The earlier surbahar and sitar was played by two or more fingers of the right hand. The mizrap or plectrum was worn on the index and the middle finger, and chikari was played with the little finger. Imdad Khan introduced the index finger-one mizrap playing for both the main string and chikari. His son Enayat Khan advocated the four right hand fingers to touch each other and not spread in the veenkar style sitar playing, followed by Barkatulla, Ashik Ali or Mushtaq Ali Khan.

This powerful jhala, straight as well as reverse (thok), of this gharana was such an advancement, that all sitar players irrespective of the gharana they belonged to, followed Imdad-Enayat's pioneering work. This was followed throughout India and remains unique even to this day. Ornamentation in the khayal style was much more intricate and skilful than the earlier sitar and surbahar. Masitkhani gath was filled with a lot of detail in meend, bol and percussion work. This was so enriched that it became as important a subject as alap with its various branches. The percussion influence, very weak in the earlier Senia sitar players, was made stronger and one could find tabla and pakhawaj tehais coming into the sitar for the first time. This was probably done with the help of Biru Mishra of Varanasi who was also an employee in the music court of Gouripur.

Imdad Khan was born in 1848 and died in 1920. He was groomed by his vocalist-sarangi-sitar-jaltarang player father Sahabdat Khan, and did not formally become anybody's disciple. The names of Nirmal Shah, Bande Ali Khan and Sahajad Mohammad is mentioned, but not formally acknowledged by the descendants today. He was a shrutidhar and could pick up anything simply by hearing. His grandson Vilayat, whose father Enayat Khan died when he was only eleven, was also blessed with this power. Imdad Khan got some material from the family of Haddu-Hassu and picked up whatever he heard from Nirmal Shah, Bande Ali Khan veenkar, Rajab Ali Khan, and Sahajad Mohammad. From Sahajad Mohammad, he learnt by listening every day—as advised and planned by his employer Raja Sourindramohan Tagore or Jatindramohan for years—by concealing himself inside a specially constructed almirah. This gave him a grasp over the Senia style details, and his son Enayat Khan, known for his goodness and honesty, told his students that his teaching will be in two parts, his own gharana in the sitar and a Senia baaj on the surbahar. Bhatkhandeji rightly observed that with all his brilliance in technique, Imdad Khan would have been an unparalleled craftsman. It was Sahajad Mohammad's comprehensive influence that made him the greatest surbahar and sitar player of his time. Equipped with unmatched technical power and command over his instruments, Imdad Khan took his concert talim from the best gharanadar musicians of his time. Like all concert-talim takers it took a generation of trial and error to enter into the dhrupadic form and that too in a handful of raags.

VILAYAT KHAN

Ustad Vilayat Khan lost his father when he was eleven. He was born on Janmashtami day in 1927 in Gouripur and lost his father in 1938. The technical base was solid and he had already made a 78 rpm in Todi. His shrutidhar ears were in search for new material which he had the capacity to translate into his sitar. In the absence of his illustrious father to guide him, the child prodigy had no alternative but to collect material from the other sources at his disposal. For reasons unknown, he does not seem to have been a favourite of his uncle Ustad Wahid Khan, who also played his grandfather's sitar baaj with great skill and virtuosity. Vilayat Khan therefore first collected whatever he could, from his father's students in Kolkata, especially Birendrakishore from whom he also got dhrupad and veena material of the Senia gharana of both sides of the Tansen lineage, the daughters and the sons.

From his mother's side he got basic khayal and thumri material from Zinda Hussain Khan and Bande Hussain Khan. He had no alternative but to go in for research and development, in quest of another style, which when magnified in a more developed sound system, would be clear and soothing. He therefore started reducing the importance of the right hand, deviated from his parent gharana, and simultaneously increased left hand meend details. This was to bring out not only the broad outlines of khayal as perfected by his father and grandfather, but all minor and major details of whatever a vocalist was capable of doing. He brought in the tanpura background by continuousely touching the joḍi before each vistar phrase. This joḍi, he made round, by using a slightly thicker gauge string. The inevitable pause and punctuations of a vocalist due to limitation of the breath span was also depicted beautifully in Vilayat Khan's sitar. He filled them up by an aesthetic use of chikari with its gandhar-pancham beauty and a number twenty-seven closed jowari Joḍi, pausing to think in this interlude, what phrase he would play next!

He had to go out to earn and support his family at an age when children would play marbles. This made him extremely practical and put into him a challenge to reach the top. This resolve was backed by long hours of practice to achieve what had not been possible in the last three hundred years of active sitar playing in this country. Among his near relatives was Amir Khansahab (who was not yet famous), Mohammad Khan (Rais Khan's father), and the music pandit and collector Dhruvatara Joshi. Vilayat drank up as much music nectar as he could from them, filtering out for his sitar only what was aesthetically relevant, and retaining the rest in his memory. From Ahmedjan Thirakwa he took the tabla peshkar ang to enrich his Masitkhani or Enayatkhani compositions. It seems that he already had in mind a model, which he gradually built up, using collected material from all sources, and fashioning these into his own mould. His technical power facilitated playing whatever could be sung, but he played only what fitted aesthetically in his sitar mould.

His music took a different shape from the early 1950s. Together with the Kolkata sitar maker Hiren Roy, he modified his old sitar made by Kanailal, made the tabli thicker and the tone rounder and more sustaining, so that he could go deeper into his now more detailed khayal style model, in which he had already replaced old style Rezakhanis with khayal mukhḍas of Faiyaz Khan, Amir Khan and Mushtaq Hussain. Naina Devi recalls he learnt with Mushtaq Hussain for some time in Delhi. Vilayat Khan used to say that he learnt from everybody but put them in his own mould. This was done with such ornamentation that the original influence was often submerged in the genius of Vilayat Khan, and became inimitable. Jñanprakash Ghosh often spoke about one composition he had made for the Boy Scouts. Vilayat picked it up immediately, but next day sang with so much decoration and ornamentation that Jñan-babu himself could hardly recognize what he had composed the day before, except for the broad outlines! This was the Vilayatkhani mould—a mould spontaneous and decorative, and beyond imitation. The transference of mehfils and baithaks to the sound system of concert halls somehow coincided with Vilayat Khan's shifting of emphasis from the right hand to the left hand. This may have been deliberate or accidental, but definitely to advantage. It was this, more than anything else, that brought out the magnificence of his sitar tone, the details of meend, and the effect of his right and left hand balance, to make him the king of modern sitar.

Vilayat Khan's music career spread over six decades. From the mid-1950s till the beginning of the following century it followed a smooth course, for his style was already developed. Between the last decade of the 1930s to the beginning of the 1950s it was a quest for style formation and editing that goes with it. This could be divided into three phases. This is clearly evident from his recordings, sometimes one totally different from the other, in approach and content.

After his father's death in 1938, the eleven year old boy could only follow and perfect what his father had taught him—some teental gaths and taans mostly following a set pattern expandable by repetition of the tail end or in parts.This continued till 1942 and even with such scanty musical material at his disposal, he shone with his unmatched clarity and speed in both fast taans and jhala. Anokhelal Mishra, the famous Varanasi tabla player known for his own speed in teental theka, was astonished at teenaged Vilayat Khan's speed and commented: 'yeh bhut kahanse a gaya' meaning that this speed with so much clarity at such a young age is beyond the reach of humans. This speed, he maintained up to his concert for King Daud of Kabul, and for this, in spite of his other great qualities, won him a Mercedes-Benz. This was delivered in India; and despite rigid controls on imported items in the mid-1960s, a diplomatic exception was made, honouring a special wish of King Daud.

After 1942 he suddenly changed his style and with other influences, a little bit of Maihar also peeped in. This may have been due to the influence of Ustad Ali Akbar Khan in his Jodhpur days, as they were great friends, and Vilayat Khan was a frequent visitor. As this did not match with his base, we somehow missed the Imdadkhani-Enayatkhani fire, though as a sitar player he still displayed stupendous skill.

When I asked him about these 78 rpm records, he said he had lost his way for some time and did not elaborate. By 1953 he came into his own again, with a rejuvenated gandhar-pancham sitar charming not just in speed but in tone and aesthetic awareness. His Mishra Khamaj, Behag, Bhatiali dhun, in 78 rpm records, and his more than two hour-long Desh for the Sadarang Music Conference (where I was present), ushered in a new form of sitar playing—not Etawa or Shaharanpur—but hundred per cent Vilayat Khan's. This endured till his last brilliant Khamaj in Mumbai a year before his death. So brilliant was his tone and sweetness that his Behag with Allarakha Khan on the tabla was accepted as brilliant in spite of a Rageshree-like elongated shudh rekhav. Incidentally, Allarakha Khan was Vilayat Khan's regular accompanist on the tabla till Ravi Shankar took him to the United States. Just prior to this, their concert in a marriage party ended in a dispute. Vilayat Khan told Allarakhasahab that he had to play with one finger to match Vilayat Khan's top speed jhala which he played with one finger. That was their last concert together. Later in life Ustad Vilayat Khan regretted this challenge and was also as apologetic about his attitude to Mushtaq Ali Khan when they played a duet in the beginning of his career in the 1940s.

Like his father, Vilayat Khan was basically a melody man and got upset whenever percussion became more prominent and disturbed the intricacies of melody. Ravi Shankar's attitude in this regard was very different. He would use the tabla to his advantage and encourage the tabalia to fill up gaps and make the total presentation richer. Ravi Shankar, like his elder brother Uday Shankar, understood show business and never allowed even his own musical personality to interfere with the smoothness, spontaneity, and commercial prospect of the combined effort. He preferred to be mentally on the same wavelength with the audience and not make his musical expressions personal or subjective in any way. It was this that made him score over the greatest musicians of the nation and made him truly international.

Vilayat Khan was very personal in his raag elaboration technique. To him, what others played did not matter, for he did not believe in standardization. When All India Radio started this, he refused to play there. According to him gradation put the genius and the hard working mediocrity together. He also believed that as long as a raag kept up the same picture and the same note importance throughout, he would accept it as correct. He often said this and his music went forward undaunted by whoever criticized it, first as 'wrong' in his formative period and then as 'different' when he became famous. This change from wrong to different was because Vilayat Khan had by then become a giant in music for his perfection, finesse, and technical command, without losing aesthetic beauty in any way—and no sitar player could match this.

STANDARDIZATION FOR UNQUESTIONED ACCEPTABILITY

Ravi Shankar went on an opposite path, ensuring that the raag interpretation was accepted by those who knew, and advocated a standardization of raags like Carnatic music and Melkarta. There was the future generation to look after, and the Vedic tradition to survive. Besides, for a musical form to become international, one has to get rid of confusing controversies and infighting. He therefore sometimes deviated from his gharana and followed what was present in Ratanjhankarji, Mushtaq Hussain, the Dagars or even Bhatkhandeji's simple guidelines. He was criticized by his own Maihar clan for this, and was given only forty per cent in the representation of Baba Alauddin Khan's music. But then, Indian music must be a little bigger than Baba and world music much bigger. Would anybody accept a Megh with shudh nikhad or a Shudhsarang with komal ni today as Baba Alauddin used to play it in true Senia tradition? I do not think so.

One Sindhura is with two nikhads, the other is with komal ni and shudh dhaivat as if the Jhinjhoti notes are now being played with a

Kafi-style komal ga. The future generation, students and lovers of music would all get confused as well with a Lalit dhaivat almost shudh or a komal ga touch in Desh. Ravi Shankar's biggest trump card was a vision of the future which could be strengthened only by a non-controversial interpretation of raags. More, because raags and their pictures have changed with time. Matanga's *Brihaddeshi* gives a totally different interpretation of this raag. The same raag in western India and in the east, follow slightly different courses. The only way out is therefore, maintaining the same note emphasis and phraseology as advocated by Ustad Vilayat Khan or a national standardization as sought by Pandit Ravi Shankar.

POPULARIZATION OF SITAR ABROAD: ROLE OF RAVI SHANKAR

In the nineteenth century Enayat Hussain played some sitar and primarily Sufi music in Europe. On the fourth anniversary of Queen Victoria's coronation, the Kolkata Traders Association sponsored a programme featuring Kaukab Khan's sarod recital, with the tabla maestro Keramatulla Khan, which received adulatory reviews. With his sarod damaged in the course of his tour, he switched over to mandolin for the last phase of his concert in Holland. Having mastered this instrument too, he played only some of the faster passages on this instrument. He also cut some 78 rpm discs on HMV, which were very popular. Baba Alauddin Khansahab and Timirbaran Bhattacharya, who composed and arranged music for Uday Shankar's dance troupe, were also known abroad for their talent. This continued till the grip of the Second World War on Europe. This may have inspired the young Ravi, Uday Shankar's younger brother, who was part of the dance troupe, and who would later play a vital role in the dissemination of Indian classical music abroad.

A hard working, punctual and meticulous person, Ravi Shankar could only get cell theatres for his initial performances in the USA

and India Friendship Societies in Europe. He worked his way up
following his elder brother, his trump cards being his virtuosity as a
sitar player, his command over raag elaboration, and his charming
personality and public relations skills. He spoke English clearly
and his power of explanation was as elaborate and precise as his
raag music formation. I was charmed several times by his music
and personality but could never imagine that he spoke so well, till I
heard him speak for more than an hour in the Mountbatten Hall
with the eloquence and totality of a seasoned orator.

George Harrison of the Beatles adored him, as did Yehudi Menuhin.
His duet with Menuhin for the United Nations was only possible
with the hard work that Shankar put in, in the several rehearsals,
for such precise melody and percussion work. This automatically
raised the status of our music, to a level much higher than that of
our Asian neighbours and made its foothold firm in world music.

Menuhin, originally an admirer of Ali Akbar Khan, shifted to Ravi
Shankar, for in him he found a more systematic and constructive
worker, knowing worldly ways more than the music-immersed
artist. The Pilu recording surprisingly had a lot of Enayatkhani
sapats played by Menuhin and the base composition was a
traditional Murad Ali Khan-Abdulla Khan-Ameer Khan one (first
taught to Sital Mukherjee, esraj player of Gouripur, and then to
Birendrakishore). Birendrakishore learnt from Ameer Khan in his
post-Rajshahi and pre-Kolkata days. Vilayat Khan also used to
play this Pilu composition but changed the *sum* to Sa instead of the
traditional Ni.

This recording, criticized by Indians and westerners alike, was a
bridge between two diametrically opposite musical disciplines. Apart
from bringing the two worlds together, it also put Indian music on
a very high pedestal in world music. The music was not a 'fusion'
as some are inclined to say but pure orthodox Indian music not

composed by Shankar but traditional to the core, assimilated and edited by him. The technical brilliance of raag and rhythm speaks highly of Menuhin's virtuosity and Ravi Shankar's ability to communicate. This, even if not for anything else, makes Ravi Shankar eligible for the highest award for spreading our heritage and for his vision of the future. No wonder Americans rushed to touch his feet in crowded Manhattan in New York. Even conservative British immigration officers stood up to take his autograph whenever Ravi Shankar entered the country. His knighthood came much later, although he would not bow to Her Majesty the Queen.

This popularity came without breaking the standardized version of the raags he played. Even a Bhimpalasi for a Canadian festival retained its purity, as much as a Darbari Kanara at the Albert Hall packed to capacity with an almost all European audience. At ninety-two he had difficulty in tuning his sitar, but still drew his usual crowd of listeners at the Barbican. A born charmer with a brilliant reflex, he continued to charm audiences, even when he was not giving a recital. His lectures would invariably be well organized, structured and edited as that by any seasoned orator or professor. He could deliver an hour-long lecture without including a single sentence on music, raag, taal, or his favourite sitar.

Ravi Shankar will be remembered for the systematic development of a raag—unhurried, detailed, and drawing out all the features of the tradition he represented. The stages are very well rehearsed and follow one another without any flaw or hesitation. This clearly points to the hours and years of systematic practice. In joḍ and its gradual speed enhancement, he displayed tremendous selfcontrol, rationality and intellect. He proved at every passage that he had not added one octave of kharaj-pancham for mere show or embellishment, but to play it as much as the main string of the sitar. He never went overboard with decorations and stayed close to the parent rudra-veena, maintaining its *silsila*, connectivity and gradual raag unfolding without jerks and jolts. He never took his audience for a ride, and his absorbed playing offered music from the treasury of his gharana to listeners all over the world. His best years was a continuous span of over three decades, after which he lost some of his sparkle with age, but always maintained the systematic, intellectual force. He became a little repetitive, but then that is the basic character of our traditional music. Besides, in today's environment of raag adulteration, pure phrases have to be hammered into the brain of the youngsters with some repetition of the distinguishing landmarks.

Nadu Mullick, his sitar maker, deserved a big applause too for making his sitar different from a Kanailal-made and a Hiren Roy-made sitar. Nadu-babu mastered the geometrical equilibrium of the fret distance in all the four strings that Ravi Shankar moved about. The fret playing was in perfect *sur* and did not have to be balanced with meend adjustment. In other words the jodi Pa fret was perfectly balanced with the main string middle octave Sa; the main string Pa balanced with jodi Re and the pancham string Dha; and this in turn again with the kharaj Re. The accuracy of the note balance in the four strings from right to left put even the piano to shame! Even the western classical musicians today agree that a large percentage of pianos played are not tuned as accurately as oft-tuned instruments like the violin, or the sitar or its parent the rudra veena.

NIKHIL BANERJEE

The surname Bandyopadhay suited this dhoti-clad bespectacled Bengali babu better than the more anglicized 'Banerjee.' A typical Kolkata man in nature and appearance, Banerjee performed the impossible task of fusing two contradictory styles in a new and highly acceptable platter. A child prodigy who won the first prize in the famous All Bengal Music Competition of the Ghosh family of Pathuriaghata when he was not even ten years old, Nikhil had the advantage of the best local teachers—John Gomes, a ganda-bandha disciple of Enayat Khan, Mushtaq Ali Khan, Radhikamohan Maitra and Birendrakishore Roychaudhuri.

After hearing Ravi Shankar in the late 1940s, his thirst for music increased manifold, and he ran to him for lessons at the Amherst Street residence of the Mukherjees where Shankar was staying as a house guest. Banerjee claimed that Shankar, always encircled by charming company, never found time to teach him, while he waited and waited. Raviji however said that he taught him Behag and Lalit—among the best performed raags of Nikhil, in his fairly large, but not too vast performing canvas of traditional raags. Nikhil Banerjee concentrated more on the madhyam vadi raags which included the Hemant Hem series (not the older Hem like Hem Kalyan but the tributaries of Hemant), and Lalit.

The person who spotted the genius in him was Birendrakishore when he together with his tabla player brother suddenly arrived without prior appointment to play for him in his 55 Ballygunge Circular Road residence. Birendrakishore advised him to go to Baba Alauddin Khan, and requested Khansahab during one of his frequent visits to the city and his house, to teach him. Alauddin Khan, in whose village Birendrakishore's father had financed the building of a mosque, could not refuse but put in a condition that his playing had to be of a particular standard. Nikhil promptly informed him of the date and time of his radio broadcast in Kolkata, which Alauddin Khan heard and promptly invited him to join the Maihar school. 'You have the power,' Baba wrote, 'but not the musical vocabulary for its expression; if you can give up worldly desires, come to Maihar.'

In Maihar, there were some intelligent students like Indranil Bhattacharjee and his own grandson Ashish, but most were quite mediocre in receiving capacity and calibre. Nikhil's entrance and his ability to grasp created enough stir to make a section of the students very jealous of him. Jealousy led to plotting and Baba was totally brainwashed by two events. Nikhil's father's letter asking him to please Baba and get the maximum material from him, was opened on the sly, and presented with colours to the old and eccentric Ustad. His playing a special Bhairavi composition in the early hours of the morning which was exclusively taught to the grandson, was the last straw on the camel's back. Shouting 'Chor! Chor!' the Ustad whipped him out of Maihar, bought him a first class train ticket to Kolkata via Allahabad and forced him to take the train. I have personally seen the whiplash marks as late as 1957, and could never forgive the two persons responsible for this. Nikhil became the world's most loved sitar player, while the other two languished in oblivion.

Nikhil was ashamed to come back to his home town Kolkata, got down in Allahabad, refunded his ticket, and bought one for Bombay to go to the kind hearted Ali Akbar. Annapurna Devi also admired Nikhil's capacity to hear and pick up immediately, and was very sympathetic and affectionate towards him as she also was aware of Baba's impulsive fits of rage. With her separation with Ravi Shankar imminent, she must have nursed a desire to make another brilliant sitar player from the technically stronger Nikhil. No wonder Ravi Shankar would often remark in good humour, 'Nikhil is Nikhil today for me!'

Ali Akbar Khan took Nikhil under his wings and played with him on the side every evening in his Colaba residence in Bombay, sharing with him the best portions of his own style, where Alauddin Khan's music peeped in, but only indirectly, and in a filtered form. Ali Akbar Khan being creativity personified, had given his father's music beautiful twists and turns—the otherwise rough and bold Maihar right hand submerged in his aesthetic and emotionally charged left hand fingertips. This, together with his fascination for the khayal gayaki of Amir Khan and its translation into sitar by Vilayat Khan, took him miles away from Maihar. No wonder when Nikhil played for the Tansen Music Conference and in the Jadavpur Music Festival after Alauddin Khan's sarod, the old man seeing the shy Nikhil touching his feet, joked, 'Oh, you have cut your hair and shaved? You should join films.' Ali Akbar Khan, the gentle colossus smiled, for he had successfully established a parallel to the best the country could boast of—and way ahead of what was being produced then, in distant Maihar.

The rest is history, for Nikhil's meteoric rise in his duets with his 'dada' Ali Akbar, as well as in solos was phenomenal. The duets forced people to give this unassuming, struggling, and hard working handsome Bengali babu a front rank status. The solos also gave him ample scope to superimpose Amir Khan's gayaki and Vilayat Khan's skilful manoeuvres on a Maihar Kharaj-pancham sitar base.

Some years later when Nikhil had already developed a unique style of his own, spontaneous and well knit, Alauddin Khan took Nikhil to his own room in Maihar after a concert in his honour, blessed him, repeating several times that he had in the past made a mistake. Maybe the saintly old man realized that theft of music is an honourable job undertaken by the talented few; and he too had done it once, when he heard the best of Rampur. In fact it was organized theft, for he offered free tea and listened to several gharanadar ustads' discussions, and demonstrations to substantiate them! His 'shrutidhar' ears recorded every detail. The moment they left, he would translate them in his sarod, rediscovering musical phrases forgotten, and remembered again. This made his music treasury full, not only with dhrupad but with khayal, sadra and tappa too. Banerjee excelled in this tappa style 'stolen' in Baba's language or learnt later from Annapurna Devi, for he was the only Maihar sitarist with a sound technical command which made this possible. He placed this novel medium-paced music exploration in meends after a very short bilambit joḍ and instantly won applause. To the listeners he was Bengal's pride, for Ravi Shankar's accented pronunciation and Benarasi ways made him more Uttar Pradesh than Bengal.

In his sitar the same obsession with Vilayat's is evident from the initial attempt of an eight stringed sitar combining kharaj-pancham with steel gandhar pancham. This failed for the intrinsic technical difficulty in managing both; but the rudra veena like the dual bridge experiment paid off for his bass kharaj ecstasy charmed Americans and Indians alike. Nikhil Banerjee's round the clock practice is remembered by the hosts who put him up in various cities and his sitar style as a whole remains inimitable till today.

He died early but will always be remembered as the country's most technically complete sitar player and one who rarely failed in a concert. Ravi Shankar's knowledge of raags and taals remained supreme. Vilayat Khan's tone and sitar virtuosity were unmatched till his death. Nikhil-da's absorbing, meditative music is missed more than anyone else's.

SITAR PLAYERS OF BENGAL

Balaram Pathak was perhaps the only sitar player who made a mark even when Ravi Shankar and Vilayat Khan were at the height of their power. His sitar tuning as well as approach to swar was so accurate and melodious that his individuality stood out in the face of such stiff competition. The echo of the tarafs resonated with each note he played in his kharaj-pancham sitar in a style as authentic as any other. His uncle Rameshwar Pathak of Darbhanga assimilated his musical matter so well that Ravi Shankar was charmed. He later admitted to enhancing his musical canvas by Pathak's elaboration technique and being influenced by his playing. Balaram Pathak later settled in Delhi, away from the sea to cure his arthritis, and received the Sangeet Natak Akademi Award for his contribution to sitar, but only in the last years of his life. Considered a *surela* genius as *khandani* as any one with the highest pedigree, the dhoti clad Balaram Pathak remained Kolkata's asset for the major part of his life.

Bhagawanchandra Das became very famous in Dhaka and used to move about in a horse-pulled landau and in great style. Together with his brother Shyamchand Das, Bhagawanchandra represented a totally different style of sitar in which the left hand middle finger was used for all notes except the starting note where the index finger was used. Born in 1852, Bhagawan Das was already a fourth generation sitar player and therefore more ancient than the Etawa gharana. He had learnt from the Senia stalwart Kasem Ali Khan, sarod player Enayat Hussain and veenkar Murshed Ali Khan. Haricharan-Chaitan-Ratan-Bhagawan-Mangal-Kartick-Niladri now make seven generations. Kartick Das (now known as Kartick Kumar) learnt from Monoranjan Mukherjee, a disciple of Enayat Khan, and later from Ravi Shankar. The gharana flavour, already lost with the Enayatkhani style in the forefront, is now under the Maihar influence. Niladri tops the fusion music circuit in the country today and plays with great virtuosity and skill.

Jitendranath Bhattacharjee was another sitar player who played the Senia sitar style in its true spirit. His approach was so professional and his talim so deep that Muslim ustads thought he was a Muslim musician disguised as a brahman. Lakshman Bhattacharjee, who belonged to the same family, was not traditional. He created a style full of tremolo, in the classical opera tradition. Though an eccentric, he was admired by the Bengali community as a genius. His 78 rpm record in Bhimpalasi can be heard by researchers in sitar music. His student Aparesh Chatterjee in turn taught dozens of students in Uttarpara near Kolkata.

Bimal Mukherjee, though influenced by Vilayat Khan's gandhar-pancham style in later years, played on a veenkar talim base, which he received from veenkar Abid Hussain of Indore. Raags therefore were at his fingertips and he could play the most complicated ones with the ease of a maestro. A very highly placed IAS officer, he played sitar with the ease of an ustad. In sadra knowledge he was supreme and had a vast repertoire.

GHARANAS AND STYLES

There has always been an obsession with gharana in our music. If it means basic styles or techniques it is acceptable. When there is a tendency to go to the extreme where a shishya is supposed to follow the guru verbatim, I must say that the character of this largely unwritten music form has been misunderstood. A reasonable percentage of playing and singing should be improvised. In the first stage of talim or lessons, these are learnt by heart and reproduced, but only to understand the movement and character, to be able to make one's own path within the set frame, in the near or distant future.This would depend on the student's creative faculty. Learning by heart is not the aim. It is a means, a stepping stone, to make the student understand the phraseology so that in future he can make phrases similar in relative note importance, and weave around them. The more the 'learnt by heart' phrases are understood and retained, the more the talim *buniyad* or learnt base.

In fixed notation music, degree of perfection in reproduction determines the musician's capacity and gives him his position in the music world. In our partly improvised music, learning by heart and verbatim reproduction can at the most make one a brilliant primary school student. The stages beyond this require a very high degree of personal talent and capacity to put the learnt material in one's own mould and reproduce with one's own creativity. If this creativity is too wild and refuses to be harnessed by the learnt material, it will degenerate to a raag fusion hotchpotch. Once the learning has really seeped into the inner retentive mind, improvisation will be guided by it, and the music will achieve that great classical height.

Let us suppose that the raag Bilaskhani Todi has been learnt, and the character of the melody has to be maintained. For this, the distinguishing phrases have to be learnt like a parrot so intensely, that the reproduction is effortless. Once this is achieved, the student goes ahead and starts building up on this base, with what he regards as not contradicting but supplementing, beautifying and enriching. He may be wrong, but pleasing. He may be right, but dry. He can be right, and beautiful, in which case he qualifies as very good. He can also be right, beautiful and different. This makes him brilliant but rebellious. The third category is usually adored by the guru. The fourth is adored by all and the musician becomes famous. With this as background can a gharana in the conservative sense survive? Abdul Karim was different from his Kirana colleagues. I remember Vilayat Khan's remark when Amir Khan described Abdul Karim's singing as 'simple.' 'Khansahab,' Vilayat Khan said, 'I can copy your singing verbatim any time, any day, but I have tried to bring out the feeling and pathos in Abdul Karim all my life, but have not been able to do so even today.'

Faiyaz Khansahab was different from his Agra colleagues, so was Bade Ghulam Ali Khan from the other Patiala stalwarts. Ali Akbar differed from Alauddin, and Vilayat differed from Enayat and Imdad. In the highly individualistic and subjective musical approach that all the greats in Indian classical music have activated, we cannot be orthodox about gharanas for gharanas themselves emerged as products of rebellion from their parent gharanas.

Mixed gharanas have come in with better communication among musicians, better transport facilities, radio, television, Youtube, etc. Like all other subjects, other gharanas are heard, appreciated or criticized in parts or whole. The appreciated parts are absorbed in the inner mind to enrich one's own musical expressions. The Indian musical tradition should be undivided and the legacy treated as a whole, and not one gharana in any way inferior to the other. Ravi Shankar's quest for raag standardization and ending differences within, was perhaps the only way to hand over our musical heritage to the more competent in the future generations without confusion and controversy.

In older times, in the absence of any link except in the grand festivals in royal durbars once a year, differences flourished even among the descendants of the same person. One in Tripura had no link with the brother employed in the royal durbar in Mysore. In the absence of documentation or notations, their sons and grandsons started drifting away both from the parent style, as well as from the remnants of the style practised by the first or second cousin living thousands of miles away. Western Indian sitar for example even looked different from the eastern ones. *Pachao ka sitar* had a different style altogether with different emphasis and different pace.This was coloured by the performers' own choices, and to humour the wishes of their landlord-benefactors. Senia 1 could be different from Senia 2 or Senia 3 in the south-west. Even sixty years ago the guru forbade his students from listening to anybody except the guru and his other students. They were warned that their focus on the style or learnt material could deviate. This might be true for beginners, but not for advanced students. Often this had its roots in the insecurity of the guru.

OUR CLASSICAL MUSIC CHANGES

When Abdul Karim Khan began his career, conservatives sneered. When he died, they wept—Alladiya Khan and Faiyaz Khan included. When Ali Akbar Khan's individual faculties started dominating what Baba had taught him, people raised eyebrows, only to hail him as the greatest in a few years. Nikhil was called 'khichri' when he combined Vilayat Khan's fast gamaks and sapats, soon to be hailed by the same group as the best. Rashid's fascination for Amir Khan and the Kirana gharana has definitely brought a roundness to his Nisar Hussain base and he is rightly hailed as the best in the country today. When the Dagars enriched by the Haddu-Hassu repertoire put in elements of fast taans in their fast jod as well as elements of instrumental jhala, the Rampur school of dhrupad made faces but in vain. Indian classical music through the ages has survived because as improvised music, it reflected the existing environment and remained evergreen. The inherent character of this music form is such that pace and punctuation as well as ornamentation details within, can change with time to suit immediate circumstances.

The two-dimensional character of the music has been maintained throughout. In spite of Bharatmuni's experiments with rudiments of harmony in his gandhargram, madhyamgram and panchamgram similar to the tetra, quatra and quintet of western music, our music stuck to its pitch, the unwavering Sa. Bharatmuni's experiments materialized fruitfully in Europe after the sixteenth century, with the coming in of harmony, polyphony and counterpoint. We had to stay in melody, for a change of Sa in the middle of playing, however well chosen, and balanced, would lead to a collapse in the raag precipice. Indians therefore worked on melody and rhythm, a two-dimensional framework similar to the two-dimensional paintings in

Rajasthani miniatures. Art and music seemed to complement each other as in the West where the post-sixteenth century three dimensional music was reflected in their three dimensional paintings.

Nature and nearness to Nature had always been the scoring point in our music comparatively free from the regimented expression of orchestras.The sun and the influence of the sun, at different times of the day was as important in Ayurveda as in our Vedic music. A time element came in, and raags were divided into *prahar*s for the different times of the day. This was believed to have a combined effect on the body and mind—the Chandini Kedara inspired by the moon, and raag Megh inspired by the rains, and together with it the eighteen varieties of the raag Malhar. Midnight peace was captured in Darbari Kanada and the festive mood in Desh.

It is interesting to note that whereas the concepts of western architecture clear the ground planning and execution whether you build a church or castle, our ancient architecture sometimes seems to come out from natural forms like the caves of Udaigiri and Khandagiri, near Bhuvaneshwar, Orissa and the scores of old fortresses one sees while travelling.

Classical western music with its highly developed and elaborate notation system is able to create something new and orchestrate with a hundred musicians—each performing his own role with superb concentration. We are more individualistic and only solo music can survive honourably. Orchestration does not fit in with the very personal approach required in raag music.

Any sustained group work in our society also becomes difficult, for the discipline and regimentation required is missing. Our ideal prayer is always in solitude and not in a congregation with others in community halls and churches. With improved transport and communication facilities, the world has become more accessible. In the obsolescence of Vedic values we live a life of mixed cultures. Mixed music and fusion have also come into vogue. Sometimes they are interesting not as a form but as an expression of individual talent. Our traditional music will perhaps try to fit in, as it has done in the past, to remain evergreen; or perhaps survive as an abode of peace in a violent, troubled world.

MUSIC THEMA

Sangeet Samrat Khansahab Alladiya Khan: My Life
Translated and introduced by
URMILA BHIRDIKAR and AMLAN DAS GUPTA

Pb. 14 x 21.5 cm. 125 pp. 42 rare b/w photographs. Rs 150
ISBN 978-93-81703-02-1

A Thema bestseller, this revised second edition of the autobiography of one of the legendary masters of Indian classical music and the founder of the Jaipur-Atrauli gharana, as told to his grandson Azizuddin Khan, includes several rare photographs, which have been added to the ones in the first edition; and a translation by Vidhushi Shruti Sadolikar Katkar of an excerpt from a chapter in Govindrao Tembe's biography of Khansahab—the only recorded account of the maestro's singing style.

Music and Modernity: North Indian Classical Music in an Age of Mechanical Reproduction
Edited by AMLAN DASGUPTA

Pb. 14 x 21.5 cm. 266 pp. Line drawings. Rs 160
ISBN 81-86017-34-8

This collection brings together essays by a number of scholars, researchers and professionals in the field of music, offering a wide range of viewpoints and approaches to the impact of modernity on the traditional practices of north Indian classical music. JON BARLOW, URMILA BHIRDIKAR, SURESH CHANDVANKAR, SIDDHARTHA GHOSH, AMELIA MACISZEWSKI, ADRIAN MCNEIL, RAJEEV PATKE, AMLAN DAS GUPTA— specialists in the fields of history of technology, instrument-making, record collection and preservation, as well as performing artists and researchers in the history and aesthetics of music—focus on the impact of technology with the introduction of techniques of sound reproduction, as also with the advent of print culture and the new values of reception and learning.

FORTHCOMING

Ustad Amir Khan, Singer Sublime: His Life and Legacy
TEJPAL SINGH
Translated from the original Hindi by MEENA BANERJEE
With rare photographs and notations for bandishes by the Ustad.

Nikhil Banerjee: Down the Heart of Sitar
SWAPAN BANDYOPADHYAY
With rare photographs, complete, annotated discography, and reviews of major concerts.